FINALLY... IT'S **YOUR** TIME TO CHOOSE A LIFE YOU LOVE

BECOMING RETIRED*ish*

A GUIDE FOR THE NEARLY OR NEWLY RETIRED

Choose the new You!
Judi Snyder

JUDI SNYDER CeFT®, CPRC

PRAISE FROM THE RETIRED*ish*

In Becoming Retiredish, *A Guide for the Nearly or Newly Retired*, Judi Snyder addresses the dilemma many baby boomers are facing today. What's next after retirement? The adjustment from who you were professionally to who you are after you retire can be a bumpy road. In her words, "Becoming Retiredish is about continuing the journey on your terms." From choosing your associations, including laughter in your life to understanding the dramatic impact that your finances have on your happiness in your later years, the book is thought-provoking and insightful.

Sharon Lechter CGMA
Author of Think and Grow Rich for Women
Co-author of Exit Rich, Rich Dad Poor Dad, Three Feet From
Gold, Outwitting the Devil, Success and Something Greater

Three months into my retirement at age 63, after being an IT professional in Corporate America for 39 years, I was fortunate to read "Becoming Retired-ish – A Guide for the Nearly or Newly Retired" by Judi Snyder. The timing was perfect! I had done my financial due diligence prior to retiring so was comfortable with my finances. However, heading into my 4th month of retirement I started to feel emotions and anxiety I couldn't put my finger on;

probably best to call it the "Oh No What Now" phase. Reading this book has been a godsend with "Aha" moments with every page turned – I felt like the author was reading my mind. I was impressed to see the book addressed the emotional side of retirement finances. I really related to the importance of adopting a "spend-shift mindset" instead of a "spend-thrift mindset" and addressed every concern I was feeling; plus it had additional financial information I hadn't considered in my initial retirement planning. I found it to be an extremely helpful guidebook of retirement advise and strategies as I determine my own personal retirement purpose.

Dorothy D., Newly Retired

This book is every bit as much a guide to reaching your greatest potential and living true to yourself as it is about retirement. While this holds immense value for anyone entering their golden years and wading into the waters of retirement, it holds an equal store of value for those of any age seeking a better understanding of who they are, what they want out of life, and how to get the most out of day-to-day living. This is a book I expect to come back to every few years to reevaluate my own purpose, beliefs, and the road forward. What's contained in this book is a set of ideas, tools, and "choosersizes" that should act as gold for anyone seeking self-discovery and a more genuine life.

Dakota P., Nearly Retired

I'm at the age when I really need to not just think about what's next, but to also start taking the steps to get there. Becoming Retired-ish surprised me, in that it's not about the actual tactics... it's about the mindset to becoming what we call "retired," so that when get there we aren't surprised with the major changes that come with.

There are so many gems in this book. The piece that struck me the most is about thinking about what I want for me, which feels strange even though this is something I thought I was already doing (joke's on me!).

Also Judi Snyder writes in depth about a different kind of ROI, and that really resonated with me. What kind of life do I want to be living if and when I'm no longer doing my livelihood? I will keep this book to reference, as it's chock full of actionable thinking strategies, which will help me put the next pieces into place. It's a roadmap for your brain. A most excellent one at that!

Sherry B., Business Consultant

I have been a stock broker for over 40 years and thought that I knew everything necessary about my own retirement plan. Judi's new book, "Becoming Retiredish" introduced a few powerful financial ideas I was unaware of and have now incorporated into my plan. It was also the first retirement book I have ever read that included a focus on non-financial areas like finding new purpose, wellness, and relationships. The integration of the financial and non-financial elements provides the blueprint for a successful and happy retirement.

Jay B., Newly Retired Financial Advisor

Wow, if I had read this book in my 30s it would have CHANGED my life.

Carolyn E., Marketing Executive

First published by Ultimate World Publishing 2021
Copyright © 2021 Judi Snyder

ISBN

Paperback: 978-1-922597-95-3
Ebook: 978-1-922597-96-0

Cover design: Ultimate World Publishing
Layout and typesetting: Ultimate World Publishing
Editor: Isabelle Russell

Ultimate World Publishing
Diamond Creek,
Victoria Australia 3089
www.writeabook.com.au

DEDICATION

This book is dedicated to my parents, John and Beverly Joseph, who gave me life and love and who were exemplary role models of positive relationships with each other and with family and friends. I am eternally grateful for my three amazing siblings, Russell, Jennifer, and John and their spouses. Together we carry on their legacy of love.

Also to my husband and soulmate, Jeff Snyder, who has given me a life I love with his unconditional love and support and who provides inspiration and a sense of adventure. I recognize his appreciation, encouragement, and celebration of my qualities that many others found intimidating.

DISCLAIMER

The content in this book is the intellectual property of Judi Snyder. You may not reuse, republish, or reprint such content without our written consent. All information posted is merely for educational and informational purposes. This book reflects the opinions and life experiences of Judi Snyder and is meant to be a guide, not gospel.

While the information in this book has been verified to the best of our abilities, we cannot guarantee that there are no mistakes or errors. Although we have made every effort to ensure that the information in this book was correct at press time, we do not assume and hereby disclaims any liability to any party for any loss, damage, or disruption caused by errors or omissions, whether such errors or omissions result from negligence, accident, or any other cause.

This book is not intended as a substitute for professional advice in the areas of mental health, diet, or nutritional programs or legal and/or financial and investment recommendations. The reader should consult their personal healthcare provider in matters relating to his/her mental or physical health, legal professional for estate planning and other legal matters and their personal financial services professional for investment or financial decisions. Should you decide to act upon any information covered in this book, you do so at your own discretion and risk.

CONTENTS

INTRODUCTION

Happiness and fulfillment in retirement are about more than money alone. Of course, money is important, but if you don't have a purpose and you aren't well, money will not make you happy. Money will make you more of what you are. Choose happy and you'll be happier. Think money will rescue you from misery, and you'll likely be more miserable.

My wish is that if you have found yourself between the covers of this book, it is out of choice and not obligation. If that is true, then congratulations, you have taken the first step to a joyful and fulfilling retirement. Choice has everything to do with your happiness. You may be nearing retirement or newly retired and panic is beginning to set in, or you may be at the height of your career and want to plan for a successful retirement at the age of your choosing. However you arrived here, I promise that you'll leave these pages with a new perspective and some new ideas.

Maybe you're counting down the days and counting up the dollars to "freedom day," or maybe it's further down the road, but the day you retire from your career will require a plan for your new purpose, wellness, and finances. If you're like most people, that day will likely come somewhere around your late fifties or early sixties. You are too young to retire your brain, too young to live on Social Security income, too young for Medicare, and not sure whether you have saved enough to have a guaranteed paycheck that you can never outlive. At the same time, you feel too old to deal with corporate politics, too old to work fourteen-hour days, and too old to continue to put everyone else first, leaving little energy for the things you want to do. The truth is, most of us never really retire these days because we are living almost twenty years longer than our parents' or grandparents' generation. The life expectancy of the average American is somewhere around seventy-eight years, give or take, and varies in other parts of the world. If you bypass the untimely causes of deaths in youth and make it to your sixties, you are likely to live well into your late eighties. In our modern era, we can spend almost as much time in retirement as we did in our working life.

These days, most people never actually retire. We reinvent life after livelihood and look to redefine our new purpose. We are moving on to our second act, third age, or whatever snazzy label we want to give it. For some, this can be starting another career, making a few extra dollars from a hobby, volunteering for a passionate cause, or simply playing golf and vacationing on a regular basis. Whatever you end up doing all day, make it a conscious choice that brings you joy and does more than fill up the hours by default.

As I look back at my life, I realize I *should'd* way more than *choose'd*. We know that annoying voice in our head all too well. Although I have no regrets, I can't help but think that replacing some of my shoulds with choices could have made a huge difference in achieving happiness sooner. Whatever becoming retiredish means to you, having a well-thought-out plan for it is the key to joy and fulfillment.

-ish
I'll meet you at seven-ish, I'm sixty-ish, I weigh 130-ish, I'll be taking a vacation June-ish, I am becoming retiredish.

INTRODUCTION

Dictionary

Search for a word   🔍

🔊 **ish**[1]
/iSH/

adverb   INFORMAL

to some extent.
"Are you busy?' 'Ish"

* https://www.dictionary.com/browse/ish

Ish is defined as "to some extent" and it's our way out of firm declarations, instead allowing us some freedom, a margin of error, for change in circumstances. Humans hate being wrong and ish is our get-out-of-jail-free card. We can feel good about our plans and still leave room for change. For the purpose of this book, "ish" will address freedom to change, freedom to embrace the transition from "should" to "choose." Transitions are ish by definition. They are not destinations, they are journeys—moving, not static. They require flexibility, continuous evolution, and adjustments over time to changing circumstances and goals. I think we can all agree our world seems to be in a constant state of adaptation or reinvention. To keep up, we must also constantly adapt and reinvent ourselves.

I believe there is an important distinction between adapting and reinventing. I see adapting as adjustment to a new norm and acceptance of societal expectation. I see reinventing as an acknowledgement of the new norm with an additional step of "making it your own," using the new norm as an opportunity to pause and ask how this new direction can bring you happiness. The look and feel are usually very different from others' expectations of how they want that to look and feel for you.

3

Becoming

Becoming anything can be challenging. Just look at a caterpillar becoming a butterfly. It's a struggle and it can be painful to watch. We want to help that tiny butterfly out of its cocoon, and yet our help will weaken the butterfly and eventually lead to its death. And so it is for humans. We need to travel along at our own pace to learn our individual lessons, sometimes excruciatingly painful lessons, but that doesn't mean we can't have a cheerleader along the way or be a cheerleader for those we love. When we finally arrive at retirement, we are greeted with a big bowl of uncertainty that comes from decades of having our lives dictated by family or financial obligations. This uncertainty hits when we are not feeling quite as sharp, healthy, or equipped to take on new challenges as we once were. You would think that by the time we reach retirement there would be an easy way to grab the golden ring of life as a reward, but no. We are left with more uncertainty and probably more life lessons left to learn on the horizon.

If you are a Boomer like me, you may be in retirement almost as long as you were in your career. This is both a blessing and a curse. The blessing? We finally get to do what we want to do; not what others expect of us or what we think we should do, and we have years of experience and expertise in our intellectual toolbox. The curse? We worry about who we will become without our career, about our health, about outliving our money, about giving it all back to Uncle Sam. We mistakenly think retirement planning is all about the money, a one-and-done thing we need to do before retiring. Few of us acknowledge that there are three stages of retirement and three main elements to consider in each of those stages; money is only one. Failure to address all three of these stages and elements may leave us unhappy, unfulfilled, insecure, and financially or physically unable to afford the bucket list we've been composing over the years.

First, understand that your retirement years are broken down into three stages: the go-go years, the slow-go years, and the no-go years. The go-go years are active. You may continue to work, start a new business, travel, volunteer somewhere, or just golf every day, but you probably won't suddenly slow down because you have left your career. Many people become more active when they have more free time to do what they want to do and are more apt to focus on a healthier lifestyle. Being more active probably requires more access to money than you were accustomed to spending when you had only a few weeks of vacation each year. The slow-go years are still active, but you begin to slow down. Your physical health may impose limitations and your energy may decline. The no-go years are mostly sedentary. For some they never arrive, but it's important to plan for them, just in case. This is the time when planning for long-term care and upkeep of your home becomes critical. In all these phases, I would encourage you to consider the purpose, wellness, and financial elements of becoming retired.

We spend our career years looking forward to retirement, but when we get there, we often find ourselves unhappy, unfulfilled, or underwhelmed. Why is this? One reason may be because for the first time we are being asked to choose what we *want* to do and not being told what we *should* do. Until becoming retiredish, we may have been sleepwalking, robotically moving through life ignoring what we choose for our best possible self. All day, every day, all we've heard until now is what we *should* do.

From the time we are toddlers to the time we retire, we are barraged by parents, teachers, family, friends, and bosses telling us what we should do. We should be walking by this age. We should be potty trained by that age. We should go to school and be proficient in "xyz" by this age. We should get A's and B's and we should go to college. We should graduate from college and get a great job. We should strive for advancement in that job. We should be a Democrat or a Republican. We should get married and have kids. Those kids should be in soccer, football, music. You fill in the blanks. This pressure is well meant and most often driven by parents who didn't have opportunities and who want to ensure that their kids do.

Should is nothing more than a detour from your authentic self and can act as an alarm. All of these *shoulds* are well meaning; if we are honest with ourselves, we recognize that we have contributed to perpetuating the *shoulds* with our loved ones. It's not entirely our fault—we've been trained to follow *should* and ignore choose, or what I define as our authentic desires. Should is the "assembly line" of life that gives us order and boundaries and that is not necessarily a bad thing; however, it is important to include your sense of self in every decision. Some shoulds are necessary and can be learned from others' mistakes. For example, you should not put your hand on a hot stove (although there is something to be said for seeing for yourself). Once your hand is burned, you are not likely to push that boundary again.

Society is patient and exceptional at influencing our behavior incrementally, step-by-step over time, as a means of grooming or indoctrination. Subliminal messages are everywhere, and we subconsciously encode those messages as our own thoughts, including these new beliefs and rules in our decision-making processes.

Edward Bernays was one of the most influential and powerful people of all time in the field of public relations and propaganda. He was

INTRODUCTION

an Austrian American pioneer, Sigmund Freud's nephew, and not widely known outside of his area of expertise. Bernays, the key advisor to five United States presidents, was considered the father of manipulation. He has been credited with being responsible for making smoking in public socially acceptable for women, among many other societal behavior changes. Bernays said:

> "The conscious and intelligent manipulation of the organized habits and opinions of masses is an important element in democratic society. Those who manipulate this unseen mechanism of society constitute an invisible government which is the true ruling power of our country. We are governed, our minds are molded, our tastes formed, and our ideas suggested, largely by men we have never heard of...it is they who pull the wires that control the public mind."

Let that sink in. Bernays rebranded *propaganda*, which had a negative and manipulative undertone, into the modern-day term *public relations*, which became so popular that today you can proudly receive a degree in PR. He identified the "secret sauce" required to tap into our innate need for safety and acceptance by society. What does this have to do with the journey from "should" to "choose"?

This process highjacked our intuitive ability to connect with our true purpose, "choose," and led us to accept "should" and the belief that serving the greater good of our tribe was more important than serving ourselves. In reality, serving ourselves first is the only way to authentically serve our fellow humans. What do they say when you board an airplane? Put your own oxygen mask on first before helping others.

Life does allow for coloring outside the boundaries of should to some extent. We hear phrases like "think outside the box" or "thought leader" to describe the person who taps into their purpose and challenges the widely accepted status quo. In fact, challenging status quo leads to growth and innovation. Although we sometimes look back on these people with admiration, the reality is that many times they were ostracized or misunderstood for their deviation from society.

To embark on the journey from "should" to "choose," we must first understand why we follow others' direction even when we intuitively feel it isn't right for us. Should is someone else's idea of how we are to behave. The minute we hear that word echoing in our brain, we must heed the alert that we are leaving the land of choice. We believe we *should* for many reasons, some good, some not so good. Humans are emotional creatures, social by nature, and we learn by observation. Conformity is a survival mechanism. If conformity becomes too far from our true self, we will either rebel consciously or sabotage ourselves subconsciously. The key is finding a way to maintain our personal integrity, honor our core values, and be a productive member of society.

Before we can begin to get back in touch with ourselves, we must be aware of the drivers that cause us to ignore our inner desires and conform. Drew Eric Whitman, in his book *Cashvertising*, defines eight common desires that represent the primal biological needs that we all feel compelled to fulfill, no matter who we are, where we live, or what we do.

INTRODUCTION

Eight primal desires in all of us:

1. Survival: a long and healthy life
2. Protection: safety, care, and protection for self and loved ones
3. Freedom: freedom from danger, fear, and pain
4. Comfort: comfortable living conditions
5. Pleasure: enjoyment of food, beverages, and experiences
6. Relationships: sexual relations, companionship, and compatibility
7. Success: feelings of superiority, being part of winning team, keeping up with the Joneses
8. Likability: social approval, being part of the "in" crowd

We will generally conform to the desired behavior that will protect and nurture these primal desires. We look for reinforcement confirming that we are safe and behaving as expected. There are both flagrant and unspoken consequences for not conforming, yet some people seem born to buck the system. We may even have times and events in our lives when we have "fallen on the sword" for our beliefs rather than conform. This appears to begin happening around midlife, hence the phrase *mid-life crisis*. The dictionary defines mid-life crisis as an emotional crisis of identity and self-confidence that can occur in early middle age. This identity and self-confidence crisis occurs when the I, our true self, gets so buried in the *should* that there is barely any semblance of who we were meant to be; we descend into depression and begin questioning everything around us. Depression, in its simplest definition, is anger turned inward. We get angry about the choices we have made and the perceived loss of who we could have been, and we begin to feel a sense of regret and awareness of our own mortality.

These eight primal desires can be summed up in two words: safety and security. In the following nine chapters, we will be exploring the primal desires as they relate to safety and security. I have grouped the material into three sections of this book: Purpose, Wellness, and Financial Security. We have a preparedness plan for almost everything we do except retirement. We think because we've completed an estate plan, we are good to go, but money and "stuff" are only one element of retirement planning, albeit an important one.

Exploring all three elements—purpose, wellness, and financial security—we will learn how to navigate the journey from *should* to *choose* in all areas of our lives. A good way to approach this excursion is by using the three R's (recognize, realize, revisit) with an open and inquisitive mind.

We must first recognize that *should* is someone else's idea of how we should behave, presented through someone else's lens. When we are more conscious of where our information and direction come from, we can be more deliberate and intentional in choosing our responses.

Recognize when you are doing something because someone else wants you to. This is the first and likely the most difficult step. Become aware of your self-talk and notice every time you say to yourself "I should." The word *should* is a warning that you are about to detour from your desire, so set that alarm to go off every time you hear it!

Realize (*real eyes*) by taking a step back and questioning the "why." Understanding the bias underpinning your own beliefs brought about by absorbing other people's biases gives you an opportunity to re-evaluate your thought paradigm. I called to check in on a client who recently became widowed to see how she was adjusting. She and her husband began dating in high school and they had been married for more than sixty years. She began our conversation by saying she was discovering so many things about herself without her "other half" that came as a complete surprise. For example, she had served oatmeal and a banana every morning for nearly sixty years. She didn't really like oatmeal or bananas, and realized for the first time that she could have something else for breakfast. Looking at things differently is not necessarily making anything or anyone wrong, it's about recognizing that something is not right for you at this time. It is about your preference. There is no "wrong" color in a crayon box, merely different colors because we are all unique. As we evolve, our desires evolve; things we used to love may change and that is okay.

Revisit your decision by asking whether this is something you *choose* to do, something you believe you *should* do, or something that you've just always done without question. Then choose and move forward. If you have been a people pleaser for most of your life, like many of us, this will require baby steps. Changing up what you want for breakfast is a great start. Working up to planning the next family vacation and all the excursions may take some time.

For some this journey can be easy and intuitive, but for most of us it requires unlearning "to follow" and relearning "to connect" to our gut instinct or inner guidance. When we reach retirement we are, for the very first time, not being told what to do every day. Everything is a choice and although that sounds great, it is often a source of our anxiety because it is new to us. Our choose muscles are weak, at best, or possibly non-existent. Choose muscles help us define our purpose and are the key to lasting satisfaction. We need to exercise the choose muscles to build them and make them strong.

It's been said the longest journey you'll ever take is from your head to your heart. This is the journey from "should" (your head) to "choose" (your heart). It is rarely an easy journey, but it is one that is necessary for your happiness and well-being. I say bon voyage, let's get this trip going!

You have brains in your head.
You have feet in your shoes.
You can steer yourself any direction you choose.
You're on your own.
And you know what you know.
And YOU are the one who'll decide where to go...
~Dr. Seuss

To get started, download the companion workbook
www.BecomingRetiredishWorkbook.com

HOOSING PURPOSE

*"Life's happenings don't create your purpose;
they reveal your purpose."*
~Judi Snyder

The Future

CHAPTER ONE

Chapter 1

ME, MYSELF, AND I

Who Am I?

Most of us have traveled through life being different people, playing different roles, adapting our identity to the situations we find ourselves in. I once attended a workshop in which the speaker asked us to take out a piece of paper and answer a simple question. Who are you? To my amazement, *all* the attendees, including myself, answered with a list of our roles. Daughter, mom, sister, executive, fur baby mom. The list was endless. Not a single person in the room simply wrote down their name as their identity. We have been conditioned to define ourselves by our roles; when those roles change, we change with them. If we don't, we are left feeling empty and confused.

When I ask people what they believe is their purpose, almost everyone answers the same: It depends on what stage of life I

15

am in. No! Your purpose is a constant, timeless, guiding driver that transcends your roles. It is a consciousness and awareness of personal values that you bring to all you do, whether that be as child, parent, employee, or friend. Your essential values rarely change. Sometimes you are not aware of their importance until there is a threat of losing them.

Abraham Maslow outlined a hierarchy of needs including physiological, safety, love, esteem, and self-actualization. You cannot progress to higher levels of the hierarchy without first having the lower needs met. For example, if you have no water and food for survival, esteem and self-actualization become less important. Freedom is a personal value that some people never thought about until the craziness of 2020 happened; they thought freedom was a given, that it would always exist, like water. Although some are fine with limited freedom, others simply cannot tolerate even the slightest infringement of their personal freedom. When we dive a bit deeper into discovering our personal values, we want to consider whether we can happily exist with or without each one as we start ranking them. This will be an important exercise because the awareness of personal core values drives all aspects of life from purpose, wellness, and financial security. For many, becoming retiredish is the first time we will think about our core values.

Life After Livelihood

I'd like to share with you the single biggest distress of Boomer retirees. Would you be surprised to learn that it is lack of purpose and fear of no longer feeling relevant? All the retirement money in the world can't make you feel happy unless you discover a new purpose and give it as much thought and importance as your

Maslow's hierarchy of needs

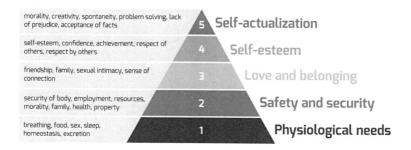

estate plan. Most people take more time planning their vacations than they do identifying a new purpose. I'm not suggesting that your purpose must be curing cancer or starting a charitable foundation. Rather, it involves purposefully deciding how you will fill your time and create a new identity when you leave your career or livelihood.

We spend much of our adult lives having our purpose determined by other people. We are either working for a company; working for customers, clients, or patients; raising children; or taking care of aging parents and family members. When these roles wane, we don't really know who we are or where our value lies. When relevancy is determined by career, we are likely to be disappointed when the career ends, even if we are counting down the days. In my work as a financial transitionist, my clients often ask this question: "Who will I be?" We are afraid of the unknown, and who we are without the title *is* the unknown. I hear comments such as these: "I'm afraid I will sit on the couch all day, watching TV, eating my way into obesity, and then die. I don't know who I am without working because I've worked since I was 14." Most of us never had to think about who we were and what brought us joy because the obligations of work and family took precedence.

One of the biggest "aha moments" for me as I became retiredish was recognizing that I measured my productivity by my stress levels. This was an observation my husband pointed out to me when I would share that I didn't feel productive no matter how much I had accomplished. I realized that the stress was somehow validating that I was being productive or valuable. If it didn't hurt, it didn't seem productive. How dare I have fun doing what I love? When I successfully recreated my life, moving from the "no pain, no gain" stress mentality to one of excitement, enthusiasm, and contentment, I was less busy and a lot more productive. We tend to confuse busyness and stress with productivity and validation. Feeling excitement is foreign, almost forbidden. So how do you tell the difference?

Stress Less, Focus More

Busyness feels frantic and hard. Productivity feels focused and smooth. Podcaster John Spencer said it best when he described *busy* as being fueled by perfectionism and *productivity* as being fueled by purpose. We have spent most of our lives trying to be the perfect "fill in the blank" and less time or no time focusing on who we are.

Busy people let others drive their progress. Productive people evaluate the pros and cons before doing something, set their focus on a goal, and evaluate their progress against that goal. Busy people say yes to everything and jump onto every trend. Productive people choose, saying yes or no based on whether their goals will be met.

Becoming Aware Is an Inside Job

First, let's examine our internal spirituality. I'm not talking about external spirituality or religious beliefs. I think most of us, by the time we are in our fifties, are comfortable with our individual beliefs, if any, in a higher power. I am suggesting we look at our internal spiritual beliefs, the core values that drive our behavior. They are the steering wheel of our gut. (And you thought "gut health" was just for your physical wellness?) It is interesting to note that as a society we have largely ignored gut health in the spiritual as well as the physical sense, and that omission has caused unhappiness and disease. We will be addressing physical wellness in section two, but let's handle spiritual wellness for now.

Internal spirituality or drivers are the values we place on God, relationships, family, peace of mind, service, bravery, professionalism, freedom, consistency. The list is long, and very personal to you. As values develop, they are crystalized and prioritized to form a values system. In essence, they form your own personal truth from which self-esteem, fulfillment, and resilience develop. Sometimes major events happen, such as the craziness around Covid-19, that highlight a value we didn't realize was so important. For example, I didn't realize freedom was so important to me until I had so many restrictions forced upon me. Revisit your values from time to time; this is never a one-and-done process.

There are many exercises on the web that you can use to determine your core values. If you are married or have a partner, this is a great exercise to do together over a glass of wine or a cup of coffee. If you are like me and my husband Jeff, you will find that your core values may be the same, but your most important value may differ. Understanding each other's internal spirituality or value system will help you to understand why we make or avoid making certain decisions and help you to determine who does what in the relationship based on your strengths and convictions. On the following two pages are the directions and a snapshot of my favorite values exercise. In my complimentary companion workbook that you can download from my website, you will find all of the "Choosersizes" listed at the end of each chapter and the link to download the workbook. I encourage you to complete each choosersize because it will help you move forward in your retiredish journey.

Now that you have your hands on the steering wheel, where do you go? It's time to create your life after livelihood. A happy and fulfilling retirement begins with determining your new purpose, replacing what I call the *should* purpose with the *choose* purpose. The enlightenment you get by doing a values exercise will help you exponentially by identifying your drivers.

What makes you happy or brings you joy? This question may be difficult to answer and it may take some time to identify. Most of us know quickly what makes us unhappy, but we don't really know what brings us joy. A great daily practice is journaling based on this prompt: "What will bring me joy today?" The practice of journaling your happy moments exercises your joy muscles daily and helps you to identify the small pleasures in front of you that would otherwise be ignored.

This exercise can start to clue you in on how to identify your new purpose so you can plan retirement activities, hobbies, and trips that fill your heart and bring you joy. So many successful life-changing people started their new ventures after the age of fifty—Henry Ford, Charles Darwin, Julia Child, Colonel Sanders, Martha Stewart, Louise Hay, and many more. Why not you? They didn't start out thinking they would change the world; they just did what they loved, and the world changed. You don't have to start a company; you may be a mentor who has a positive influence on only one person, and that may be the person who ends up changing the world!

How to determine your values?

ep 1: Identify your top values

o through the list of words and circle every word that resonates with you. Don't put any limitations 1 how many words you circle, just circle the word that best captures the essence of you. Circle least ten and if there are similar words, for example, philanthropy and generosity, ask; do you nd to help friends and family (generosity) or volunteer for causes that are important to you such fostering animals or volunteering at a food bank (philanthropy). They can be distilled into the e that resonates with you the most.

ep 2: Prioritize your top values

s step is probably the most difficult because you'll have to look deep inside yourself. It's also the ost important step, because, when deciding, you'll have to choose between solutions that may tisfy different values. This is when you must know which value is more important to you.

gin narrowing down the list to five words in no particular order by asking "if this but not that" or other words once you've narrowed down the list, look at the first two values and ask yourself, "If ould satisfy only one of these, which would I choose?" It might help to visualize a situation in iich you would have to make that choice. For example, if you compare the values of service d stability, imagine that you must decide whether to sell your house and move to another untry to do valuable foreign aid work, or keep your house and volunteer to do charity work ser to home.

ice you've chosen one of the two, put that into another list. Proceed by comparing the word u didn't choose (second word) to the third word, writing that choice in the paired down list. ep working through the list, by comparing each value with each other value, until your list is in e correct order.

p 3: Reaffirm your values

eck your top-priority values, and make sure they fit with your life and your vision for yourself.

- Do these values make you feel good about yourself?
- Are you proud of your top five values?
- Would you be comfortable and proud to tell your values to people you respect and admire?
- Do these values represent things you would support, even if your choice isn't popular, and it puts you in the minority?

ice you have your top five values, arrange them in order of importance. You may find that ne of your values change or modify depending on life situations and current events. Sometimes u don't realize something is an important value until it is "threatened." If you have a partner, do with them so you can understand each other's driving values.

edit: James Manktelow and Rachel Thompson, creators of www.MindTools.com, a website ere people could learn what it takes to become a successful and effective leader.

VALUES EXERCISE WORDS

Accountability	Excitement	Originality
Accuracy	Expertise	Patriotism
Achievement	Exploration	Perfection
Adventurousness	Expressiveness	Philanthropy
Altruism	Fairness	Positivity
Ambition	Faith	Practicality
Assertiveness	Family-orientation	Preparedness
Balance	Fidelity	Professionalism
Belonging	Fitness	Prudence
Boldness	Fluency	Quality-orientation
Calmness	Focus	Reliability
Carefulness	Freedom	Resourcefulness
Cheerfulness	Fun	Restraint
Clear mindedness	Generosity	Results-oriented
Commitment	Goal-orientation	Safety
Community	Goodness	Security
Compassion	Grace	Self-actualization
Competitiveness	Gratefulness	Self-control
Consistency	Growth	Selflessness
Contentment	Happiness	Self-reliance
Continuous Improvement	Hard Work	Sensitivity
Contribution	Health	Serenity
Control	Helping Society	Service
Cooperation	Holiness	Shrewdness
Correctness	Honesty	Simplicity
Courtesy	Honor	Spontaneity
Creativity	Humility	Stability
Curiosity	Independence	Strategic
Decisiveness	Ingenuity	Strength
Dependability	Inner Harmony	Structure
Determination	Inquisitiveness	Success
Devoutness	Insightfulness	Support
Diligence	Intelligence	Teamwork
Discipline	Intellectual Status	Thankfulness
Discretion	Intuition	Thoroughness
Diversity	Joy	Thoughtfulness
Effectiveness	Justice	Tolerance
Efficiency	Leadership	Traditionalism
Egalitarianism	Legacy	Trustworthiness
Elegance	Love	Truth-seeking
Empathy	Loyalty	Understanding
Enjoyment	Making a Difference	Uniqueness
Enthusiasm	Mastery	Unity
Environment	Obedience	Usefulness
Equality	Openness	Vision
Excellence	Order	Vitality

> *Discovering your guiding values allows you to understand your past behavior so you can unlock future joy and happiness.*
>
> ~Judi Snyder

Choosersizes – It's All About Me!

🐚 List all the old ways you defined yourself and create a list of new definitions you want to consider.

🐚 Identify your internal drivers by doing the Values Choosersizes in the companion workbook.

🐚 Journal about things that bring you joy and gratitude.

*Download the companion workbook
www.BecomingRetiredishWorkbook.com

Chapter 2

YOU'LL SEE IT WHEN YOU BELIEVE IT

The real voyage of discovery consists not in seeking new landscapes, but in having new eyes.

~Marcel Proust

Never Shake a Tablecloth Outside in the Evening

Back in the eighties, I was invited to my friend's Italian "feast of seven fishes" Christmas Eve celebration. If you've ever been to one, you know it is full of all kinds of delicious Italian food, and of course scrumptious crusty Italian bread. At the end of the evening, while I was helping clear the dishes, I rolled up a tablecloth covered with crusty bread crumbs and headed toward to the door to shake it outside. Aunt Lucy frantically came running after me and bellowed, "Dear, *never* shake a tablecloth outside in the evening." What? Aunt Lucy proceeded to tell me. "It is bad luck to shake a tablecloth when it is dark, we need to leave this for the morning sun." *Okey-doke*, I left it rolled up for the morning.

Fast forward some forty years later. I was carrying groceries in from our garage through the laundry room. Some leaves had blown into the garage, and I had tracked some of them into the laundry room onto the throw rug. When I finished putting the groceries away, I rolled up the rug, opened the door to shake it outside, and noticed it was dark. And just like that I stopped dead in my tracks, backed away from the door, and left it until morning. I wasn't going to bring any bad luck my way!

The next morning, when I saw the rug rolled up, I recalled Aunt Lucy sharing her "bad luck tablecloth" tale and had an "aha moment." Aunt Lucy, who I had met only once forty-plus years ago, had told me an old wives' tale that I had heard only once. Unconsciously I had remembered that tale, and I had expanded the tale of the tablecloth with breadcrumbs to include a throw rug with dried leaves—and that tale stopped me dead in my tracks. I had imprinted a superficial, insignificant tale deeply into my belief system, convincing myself that my action would bring bad luck. The tale emerged and drove my behavior without a single conscious thought some forty years later.

Remember the eight primal desires we discussed in the introduction? One of the reasons this insignificant tale imprinted my belief system so powerfully is that it threatened my safety and security. Bad luck became a threat to one or many of my primal desires. What insignificant (and significant) limiting beliefs are still driving you? Are they nonsense? Most of our beliefs come from mirroring others' behavior and hearing certain stories and phrases repeatedly. Imagine how entrenched they can become when they are reinforced by those we love and with whom we spend much of our time. Who is your Aunt Lucy? What are your "tablecloths"? What unconscious beliefs have you picked up that are holding you back? We all have them; after all, we are human. The more primal desires are threatened—safety, security, need to be loved, social acceptance, comfort—the more deeply entrenched the belief.

These unconscious beliefs influence our behaviors and affect our outcomes. Research shows that 95 percent of our behavior is unconsciously motivated. Yes, that isn't a typo, you read that correctly. I'll repeat, 95 percent of our behavior is unconsciously motivated. That means that only 5 percent of our cognitive behavior or awareness is conscious. Many neuroscientists have shown that most of our decisions, actions, emotions, and behaviors depend on the 9 percent of brain activity that lies beyond conscious awareness, meaning that 95 percent (or even as much as 99 percent) of our lives are determined by the programming in the subconscious mind. Dr. Bruce Lipton, former professor of medicine at Stanford University, says the new science of epigenetics has shown that our genes are, in fact, controlled and manipulated by how our minds perceive and interpret the environment. Dr Lipton's view is that if we interpret things in a positive way, we start living healthier and better-quality lives. It is a bit startling to think that many of our decisions, emotions, actions, and behaviors happen without deliberation. To become more aware of our behavior, let's unpack the various types of limiting beliefs and biases.

"*Whatever meaning you give to an unwanted outcome or event is the clue to the underlying belief.*"

~ *Judi Snyder*

Wikipedia identifies 104 biases. Because discussing all 104 biases would be overwhelming, let's look at how they are categorized. I prefer the way strategic communicator Travis White in his publication *How Many Cognitive Biases Are There?* January 12, 2018, has broken biases into four grouped categories:

Too much information. We notice things already primed in memory. We notice (and remember) vivid or bizarre events. We notice (and attend to) details that confirm our beliefs.

Not enough meaning. We fill in blanks from stereotypes and prior experience. We conclude that things that we're familiar with are better in some regard than things we're not familiar with. We calculate risk based on what we remember (such as vivid or bizarre events).

How we remember. We reduce events (and memories of events) to the key elements. We edit memories after the fact. We conflate memories that happened at similar times even though in different places, or memories that happened in the same place even though at different times, or with the same people, for instance.

The need to act fast. We favor simple options with more complete information over more complex options with less complete information, or simplicity of completion. We may experience inertia. If we've started something, we continue to pursue it rather than change direction even though the new option may better serve us.

Although there is a lot to say about biases, the specific biases I would most like to focus on are *confirmation bias* and *bandwagon bias*. I believe these are the two most important and relevant to the *should* versus *choose* mentalities. These biases, once you are aware of them, can be easily recognized and will impact your overall retiredish happiness.

Confirmation bias arises when we allow our past and unconscious or subconscious belief systems to take over the steering wheel of our actions. These biases make us feel uneasy and create tension, because they go against our core values and what we feel in our gut. Cognitive dissonance is the state of having inconsistent thoughts, beliefs, or attitudes, especially as it relates to behavioral decisions and attitude change. It kicks in when we become aware of new information that conflicts with old ideas. It goes something like this: We have a longstanding belief, new information is introduced, we feel discomfort and confusion, so we tend to rationalize or explain things away, rejecting the new information that conflicts with our existing beliefs. We simply cannot allow ourselves to believe the new information is true, so we will search until we find information that support our old beliefs. And guess what? We will always find information that will support any belief. We live in an age where the internet can provide documentation on every point of view imaginable, regardless of how far-reaching this information can be. Furthermore, we can always find an expert who will support our bias.

Next, consider bandwagon bias, or the desire to be part of the group (also called herd mentality). If we are being honest, we all want to be a part of something bigger than ourselves and there is nothing wrong with seeking inclusion. Where it gets tricky is when it makes us uncomfortable and we get that warning sign in our gut, the feeling that I *should* because if I don't something will happen. Few of us will ever forget 2020 and the obscene amount of change that occurred in an instant. One of those changes that may have happened gradually over time, but suddenly became glaringly obvious in 2020, was "cancel culture." It is no longer acceptable to be human and forgiven for your mistakes. We are relegated to a life of apology and repentance.

Any mental health professional will tell you that their practice tripled throughout 2020. Why? I believe it was because our need for belonging was in conflict with our intuition or innate beliefs. We risked losing love, friendships, jobs, even our homes, if we dared to think differently. All our primal desires were threatened. Being politically correct used to be somewhat humorous and satirical and suddenly it was a requirement for essential living and having our basic needs met. To complicate matters further, the goal posts kept shifting. Words were being redefined, along with food labels, entertainment, and even the names of sports teams. What used to be politically correct a year ago is now taboo.

When you combine confirmation bias with bandwagon bias, it can become difficult to change your beliefs. Welcome to the comfort zone—the graveyard of innovation, the proverbial couch potato of thought. If we fail to develop critical thinking skills to stretch our imagination, much as we would get up off the couch to take a walk, our mind will become lazy and unhealthy just as our body would. As difficult as it may seem, updating your belief system to one of *choice* rather than *should* will ultimately make you happier and more fulfilled.

How The Heck Do We Navigate This New Paradigm?

We acknowledge the fear. We acknowledge the threat to our primal drivers. We recognize our fear, and understand that fear is steering the bus. Fear is nothing more than the emotion we get when we are going against personal truth, against what we know is true for us, and the recognition that it is vastly different from what is being asked of us. How do we determine when it's time to take back the steering wheel and when it's worth the risk? It begins with being uncomfortable and progresses to being unbearable. At some point we reach a breaking point and blow. Most of us must be pushed to this point. As the saying goes, "Life will give you a whisper, a roar, or a two-by-four." It is your choice. The key to being happy is recognizing the zone in which you are uncomfortable (the whisper) and making a mindful decision before the unbearable (the two-by- four) sets in.

When you are acting in concert with your core values, it may make you uncomfortable but not so much that you are willing to risk not being you. By the time we reach retiredish age we have many battle wounds from the two-by-fours. Wouldn't it be nice to learn from the whisper and not the two-by-four?

When Life Gives You a Dilemma, Make Dilemmonade

How do we listen for the whispers? If we look back at any decision we now define as a mistake, we can probably agree that in hindsight, we overlooked some warning signals. The challenge is recognizing those warning signals and intercepting our behavior before we make a mistake. To do this, we must learn to respond rather than react. Responding requires forethought, taking a step back, and not acting on impulse. Reaction, on the other hand, is impulsive, acting out of reflex as I did when I was stopped dead in my tracks because of Aunt Lucy's old wives' tale about shaking a tablecloth at night. I'm grateful to Aunt Lucy because, had it not been for her tale forty years ago, I wouldn't have had my aha moment and recognized how much impact even the simplest and most benign statements, heard only once, can have on behavior. Aunt Lucy and her tale led me to develop my process for belief transformation.

Be-leave:
Be willing to explore old beliefs,
Leave those which no longer serve your happiness.
~Judi Snyder

We can identify and transform these unconscious beliefs if we choose to challenge our personal status quo. It won't happen overnight; it is a process like everything else having to do with our emotions. First, we need to identify the obvious behaviors that we want to change. As we discussed earlier, journaling is a great way to begin.

Give an IOTA About Your Beliefs

IOTA is a process I developed to help me look at my own beliefs and I believe it will help you. An *iota* refers to something very small. Although our belief systems are huge, our knowledge of them is very small and it hides in the crevices of consciousness. Uncovering these limiting beliefs will diffuse difficulty and infuse joy into your life.

The IOTA process includes four simple steps:

1) Identify the meaning you give to an unwanted outcome. That is the clue to the underlying belief. Are your behaviors coming out of *inspiration* or *obligation*?
2) Observe your actions. Are they consistent with what you say you want?
3) Travel down both "what if" roads: What if I do? What if I don't?
4) Ask questions:
    a. Is this true? (Example: money doesn't grow on trees.)
    b. Why do I believe this to be true? (Example: money isn't abundant.)
    c. What would I prefer to believe/reframe? (Example: money can grow like a tree.)

To help us move through this process, let's look at a common example many of us may have heard as kids.

Identify the limiting belief: Money doesn't grow on trees, it's hard to make money, romantic love only happens in Hallmark movies.

Observe your actions: Are you working on the steps to make money or are you doing things that keep you busy but don't actually do anything to advance your business or your job position? Are you taking initiative to learn the latest and greatest advances in your business, stepping up for projects, or continuing your education for a different business if you want to change your field? How about your relationships? Are you investing time with your partner to keep on top of what makes each of you happy or merely coexisting as roommates? Are you focusing on their faults and not on their beautiful attributes that led you to fall in love in the first place? Let's look at a different scenario: I always lose money no matter how I invest it. Everyone else seems to make money on their investments; I always get ripped off. Ask yourself these questions: Did you do the due diligence for your investment, or did you just listen to a friend who told you why, where, and how to invest? Did you plan what you wanted to accomplish with your money, or did you get caught up in an emotional investment because it was great for the environment or because your best friend was starting a new business that could not fail? Just as we need to understand our purpose, we need to know the purpose of our money. We will dive deeper into this in the last section.

Travel down the "what if?" road. What would happen if you volunteered for a project that isn't part of your job but that would stretch your skills? What if you applied for a job completely out of your experience or skill set? What if you didn't? What if you made less money doing something you love but had more time to spend with friends and family? What if you stayed with your partner? What if you had a designated date night? What if you learned your partner's "love language"? What if you just kept coexisting as roommates? What if you parted ways? What if you explored new ways of investing your money that you hadn't thought about before and that allowed you to work less? What if you didn't because it makes you uncomfortable to open your financial statements?

Ask whether it's true. Is it really true that others advance in their careers who do just as much work as you? Are you really taking initiative to learn cutting edge performance and profit processes? Do you really know others make money and you don't? Are you really putting the time in with your financial professionals to understand how to multi-task your money? Are you taking the time to understand and become aware of the things you do because you think *you should* rather than *you choose*? Here is a big one: Do you truly love your partner or are you just afraid to be on your own?

In chapter five we will dive deeper into relationships. We will cover rationalization and blame and how they are lethal to any relationship. Our relationship with ourselves is the first and most important of all relationships. We must begin with love and kindness toward ourselves first and take personal responsibility for our results. When we go through the IOTA process, rationalization and blame start to surface. It is hard to take personal responsibility and even harder to change years of behavior. We can't change what happens to us, but we can change how we respond and move through what happens. If we want a different result, we must do things differently. Einstein said it best when he observed, "You can't solve a problem with the same mind that created it."

We can transform unconscious limiting beliefs into empowering beliefs by working through the IOTA process. Stress is the result of a conflict between desire and belief. Stress is the main obstacle to this transformation. Let's look at a functional MRI study, which measures the activity of the brain and its response to stimuli. *Raichle, Sheline, and colleagues (2009) identified a group of individuals whose brain images indicated that they were unable to "lose themselves" in work, music, exercise, or other activities that enable most healthy people to get "outside" of themselves. Interestingly, it turned out that

---

*What Neuroscience Reveals about the Nature of Business Jeffrey L. Fannin, Ph.D. and Robert M. Williams, M.A. Center for Cognitive Enhancement, Glendale, AZ 85306

these were highly stressed, depressed individuals, people whose emotions and thinking maladaptively colored their response to their environment, the task at hand, or the people around them. Raichle's results also found that our ability to maintain effective relationships with others begins with a healthy relationship with our inner self and our relationship to our own thoughts, beliefs, and emotions. But the good news is, you can let stress be the barometer to signal when changes need to be made. Our desires and beliefs must be in alignment, or you'll never get your desires.

Choosersizes – What You Think About, You Bring About

🐚 Using the "Limiting Belief Choosersize" in the workbook, begin to journal your limiting beliefs.

🐚 Identify the irrational "Aunt Lucy" beliefs or tales that threaten your primal desires of safety and security.

🐚 Using the IOTA process, take the trip down a few of your limiting beliefs and transform the outcome to one of your choice.

*Download the companion workbook
www.BecomingRetiredishWorkbook.com

Chapter 3

NOW WHAT
DO I DO?

Now that we have addressed our inside journey, let's take some time to navigate our outside journey. The conventional view of retirement would have you believe you'll be sipping umbrella drinks on the beach in between shuffleboard games, then heading off to the early-bird special of the day at your favorite diner. Although that may be what you do on a day or two when you become retiredish, it is certainly not the new norm. Boomers have forever changed that archetype.

Whether you are an employee, an entrepreneur, a volunteer, or a retiree who just wants to make a few extra dollars, you can monetize your talent and expertise. Too often we sell ourselves short and take for granted our gifts. You know those things we do that others say they would "kill" for? Gifts are a funny thing. They come so easily for us that we often don't recognize their innate value. Yet, when we are performing or living our gift, it is timeless and magical. Whatever our gift is, someone wants to know how we do it, how to do it better, faster, cheaper, or more streamlined. Our gifts are born and revealed from life's trials and tribulations.

When we learn how to embrace those things and ask how we can learn from this, we begin to see the personality of our gifts emerge. When we begin to contemplate how we will be spending our newfound time, knowing our gift can give some direction.

We've all heard about bucket lists, which tend to be travel and money driven. Heck, there have even been movies about them! As we've learned from the Covid-19 era, it isn't always feasible to travel. Travel can be challenging during these times of restriction and living on a fixed budget may limit our ability to fulfill our travel dreams by jetting off to bucket-list destinations. Get creative and embrace new ways of experiencing new places and replace your time with experiences that bring joy. What paths can your mind travel down that will enhance your well-being?

Ditch the Bucket and Be Curious

When I think of a bucket list, I think of travel and money. The times we are living in now prohibit many types of travel even for people who have the money. Robert Laura, from The Certified Professional Retirement Coach program, suggests you consider developing a "curious list" instead. By writing a curious list you free yourself to take adventures in other ways. What is a curious list? It is, simply, a list of things you want to learn more about. It is about exploring something new, such as learning a language, rather than vacationing to a new destination. Adding brain teasers to your curious list will keep you mentally sharp. Perhaps you always wanted to learn how to make pastries but never had the time, or maybe you would like to master a three-course Italian meal? Did you ever want to learn another language? Did you know there are apps for your cell phone that can teach you just about any language you desire? Where are some of the places you always wanted to travel? Did you know you can take virtual tours of these places? Do a quick search on your favorite search engine for the 15 best virtual tours and you get enough ideas to keep you busy for months. Consider hosting a virtual travel tour party or cooking class for your friends or family. You may decide mentoring a young adult or volunteering at the food bank would be fun—you are limited only by your imagination. Maybe you can start a home business for some extra dollars while having boatloads of fun in your yoga pants.

Becoming retiredish is about continuing the journey on your terms, with a full tank of gas!
Curiosity fuels the engine of creativity, joy, and gratitude.

~Judi Snyder

Making Dough with What You Know

Make a list of all your special talents, hobbies, and contributions. Once you make a list, think of ways you can turn that list into some extra dollars or pay it forward by helping someone just beginning their work journey. You may write a book, develop an online course, video class, or webinar on topics of your expertise or hobby, start a podcast, and share your gifts with the world. Others may have similar training, skills, or experiences, but no one has the combination you bring to that training, skill, or experience. Just as no two snowflakes are exactly alike, so it is with humans. We all have different perspectives that enable us to see the same object or situation through a different lens. Don't take yourself for granted or minimize your value.

People need what you know how to do. Once you have created a product, re-purpose that content into many different packages (for example e-books, Kindle books, video courses, podcasts, speaking engagements, online and offline newsletters, coaching packages). The options are endless. There is always someone who needs to know what you do and how you do it.

People solving problems is how all innovation is born. Airbnb began because a couple of financially struggling college kids needed money for rent and knew that their budget-conscious friends needed lodging that was cheaper than expensive hotels and cleaner than seedy motels. And just like that, a couple of college kids with an air mattress gave birth to a 31-billion-dollar company. What problem do you wish could be solved?

Another example of creative reinvention involves an artist who, upon being retiredish, found herself taking long walks on the beach. She noticed trash scattered here and there and began picking up the trash every morning on her walks. She began incorporating the trash into her artwork and "Trashformation" was born. She now creates *amazingly* beautiful artwork from discarded beach trash, she participates in a global environmental movement, and she gets her daily walks in while she's at it. Another woman purchased a high-end camera and began taking photos of her favorite sport, wind surfing, and turned them into greeting cards.

Here are more examples of ways to make some extra "cha-ching": career coaching in your field, secret shopping, serving as a mock juror or virtual assistant, adding an Airbnb room in your house, babysitting, dog walking, internet marketing, selling stuff on eBay or Etsy, offering handyperson services, cooking, running errands, tutoring, coaching, or being a referee. There may be people doing these jobs already, but can you put a unique spin on the way that job is being done? Contact some temp agencies and see what part-time offerings they may have that sound interesting. This allows you to try different jobs with no long-term commitment. Earning an extra couple hundred dollars a month can have a profound effect on your financial future. A couple hundred dollars a month could build up to become a vacation fund that helps you check off your travel bucket list. Or it could be the difference between dipping into savings and having more funds available when you are older or have less desire or ability to work. Did you know that most bankruptcies could have been prevented with just an extra $500 a month?

A funny thing happens with your brain when you ask a question. Questioning will help you dig deep into that subconscious of yours and deliver the answers. Isn't it better to ask positive, forward-thinking questions so you get the positive answers? Here are some questions that you can ask yourself to begin thinking about your new purpose.

Gifts List

1) What is it you like to do so much that time flies by when you're doing it? We all know those times when we forget to eat, or look up from a project and realize it's dark outside.
2) If money were no object, what would you do all day?
3) What do people pay for that you do easily? What do people say you do really well?
4) What do your friends and family always seek your advice on? What do you take for granted that you can do that others have difficulty doing?
5) What have you always wanted to do but never had the time for?

Choosersizes – Find Yourself by Giving Service to Others

🐚 Develop a "curious list."

🐚 Complete your "gifts list."

🐚 After completing a gifts list, jot down ideas on how to "make dough with what you know."

*Download the companion workbook
www.BecomingRetiredishWorkbook.com

HOOSING WELLNESS

"Optimal wellness is managing your mind while minding your body, nurturing your soul, and creating joy.

Joyfulness is shedding the should and embracing the choose in every aspect of your being."

~Judi Snyder

Chapter 4

ARE YOU TRAINING YOUR DOGMA OR IS YOUR DOGMA TRAINING YOU?

Dogma is defined as a principle or set of principles laid down by an authority as incontrovertibly true. Wait, didn't we just spend an entire section discussing internal values, looking at limiting beliefs, and questioning what is true? Section one of this book was devoted almost entirely to our mind and spirit, our internal spirituality and values that drive our behavior. We learned how to identify our values and recognize limiting beliefs that no longer serve us. Perhaps dogma created those beliefs. We developed our beliefs 95 percent subconsciously and some of those beliefs may interfere with our optimal wellness. Dogma is neither good nor bad, it just is. Its effect on our wellness depends on whether it is a product of our own conclusion or whether it is adopted out of fear, pressure, the need for acceptance, or default. There is dogma around all behavior, and that includes diet and exercise.

In section one we focused on inner fitness, understanding the origin of our beliefs, and becoming aware of the dogma that drives our behavior. The management of our beliefs is the key to optimal wellness. Beliefs are neither good nor bad until you ask yourself one simple question: Are my beliefs acting as a leash around my proverbial neck, holding me back from running free to catch the frisbees of life? Are they holding me back from being my best, most happy and healthy self? Am I consciously honoring my internal spiritual values to please myself or someone else? In this section on wellness we will examine how to manage those beliefs with realistic expectations for our body, mind, and spirit. We will merge the wisdom we have accrued during our lives with the natural progression of our aging bodies and embrace realistic expectations.

Diet and exercise are the first things we think of when someone says "wellness," yet they are only two components of true wellness. We throw the word wellness around to include anything to do with physical health, but the fact is, wellness has just as much to do with the health of our mind and soul. I did a survey of people aged 45 and over, asking how they define wellness. Surprisingly, I got basically the same answers from most of them, give or take some age nuances. Almost all responses included mental health, happiness, and contentment along with physical health, and a few included financial health. In this section we will be learning how to take a self-care sabbatical, probably something many of us have never done before. Self-care involves inner fitness as well as outer fitness. The two must work in harmony together for optimal health.

The Waist Is a Terrible Thing to Mind!

The most important part of being a vibrant human is your health and well-being. If you don't have your health, you cannot pursue joy no matter how wealthy you may be. A favorite quote from Roger Landry, MD, MPH, is "live long, die short" and he has written a book with the same title "Live Long, Die Short: A Guide to Authentic Health and Successful Aging." Dying is inevitable, but quality of life is largely controllable. Living longer is great if you feel good but dreadful if you don't.

Physical health is much easier to systematize than mental health. We can follow a specific diet and exercise regimen and we are promised a specific result. What isn't always clear is that results are based on the foundation from which we begin. We make assumptions that what has worked for us in our youth will work once again as we age. This is mostly not the case. Although I'm not an expert in either dieting or exercise, my intention is to bring some new ideas and awareness of some considerations as we age. I suggest choosing what resonates with you and doing a deeper dive into those areas with the appropriate experts and authorities.

What we eat, our diet, becomes even more important as we age than it was when we were young and burning the candle at both ends with few negative impacts. As we get older, our pancreas gets tired and unable to process sugar or carbohydrates as efficiently as when we were younger. This can lead to hormonal changes, diabetes, pre-diabetes, or insulin resistance that can cause us to feel lethargic and even confused. Whatever diet or way of eating you choose, you may want to consider lower-carbohydrate foods, and make the carbs you do eat count by choosing healthy vegetables, legumes, and fruits that are nutrient rich. Eliminate processed foods as much as possible by sticking to the outer isles of the grocery store. You may also consider adding supplements or a multi-vitamin to your daily routine. I'm not a doctor, so I always recommend consulting your physician before taking any supplements or implementing any dietary changes. Your doctor will know your health conditions and be able to recommend the best supplements and way of eating for your optimal health. Getting regular physicals can reveal hormone deficiencies that can creep up with age. Women as well as men may develop a sluggish thyroid requiring medication. Women may need progesterone or estrogen supplementation and men may need testosterone supplementation and/or medication, which can make a world of difference in energy and mental acuity.

My personal experience was a frustrating, discouraging, and expensive five-year journey. I finally found what worked for me by paying big bucks for a concierge physician who took the time to evaluate my food and exercise log. I was eating all the right foods, exercising, and staying within my calorie range, yet I was shedding *zero* pounds. I was 85 pounds overweight and in the "I've been on a diet for two weeks and all I lost was fourteen days" mode." It has taken me a long time to be able to say that out loud, let alone broadcast it in my book that the masses will read.

My physician introduced the concept of insulin resistance and suggested I think not only about what I was eating but also about *when* I was eating. Huh? For about five months I consumed as much information as I could read about insulin resistance, and it made a huge difference in my weight, energy, and mood. WebMD defines insulin resistance as when cells in your muscles, fat, and liver don't respond well to insulin and can't use glucose from your blood for energy. To make up for it, your pancreas produces more insulin. Over time, your blood sugar levels rise. Your bloodwork may appear normal or could indicate pre-diabetes. One tell-tale sign is weight around the belly. You almost certainly have insulin resistance when you have belly fat.

In my early life as an athlete, I was taught to eat five small meals a day so I could keep my metabolism burning. Although this worked for me as a young athlete when my pancreas was operating at optimal condition, it didn't work for me as a 58-year-old woman. You see, every time you eat anything, you spike your insulin. When you spike your insulin, you don't burn carbs as efficiently because your aging pancreas is tired. With two small changes—limiting carbohydrate intake to healthy veggies and lower-carb fruits such as berries, along with intermittent fasting—I was able to shed 85 pounds. It didn't happen overnight—it took about eighteen months. I've been able to maintain my healthy weight since 2018 with minimal effort and still enjoy life. I'm not suggesting and certainly not prescribing you shed your pounds this way, rather I'm inviting you to shed your old way of thinking and doing and be open to learning new ways of getting healthy. Do your own research, feel what resonates with you, and get your physician's blessing.

Most people believe that exercise, or lack thereof, is the primary factor in weight control, but our way of eating determines 80 percent of the results. If you take away anything from this chapter, please consider implementing a healthier diet. There are loads of books, research papers, apps, and YouTube videos on healthy eating that can educate you on the latest research and programs.

Get into the Groove by Starting to Move!

If exercise impacts only 20 percent of our weight control, why should we care? Because exercising works. A Harvard Alumni Study, *Exercise intensity and longevity in men*, suggest that men who exercise regularly can gain about two hours of life expectancy for each hour of exercise. But how much exercise is enough? Organizations such as the Centers for Disease Control and Prevention suggest 30 to 60 minutes of moderate to vigorous walking five days a week. The risk of all sorts of disease, especially diabetes and cardiovascular disease, is almost halved in people who follow a regular exercise routine, and this may increase life expectancy about five years longer on average compared with inactive people.

As we age our eyesight, hearing, and mobility may decline. This doesn't mean we stop tending to our health and exercise just because we can't do it the same way we once did. We can find alternatives, adjust, and most of all make it fun. For example, if you have knee issues you can replace tennis with pickleball, go kayaking, take a yoga or Pilates class rather than running a half marathon, or even get out into nature and ride a bike.

Staying active is important for bone density and heart health, which makes all the difference in how we feel as we age. What good is living longer if we are in pain and can't walk? Two of my favorite exercise hacks that helped me stay active and accountable are my fitness tracker and streaming subscriptions. I walk 45 to 60 minutes a day on the treadmill. While I'm walking, I watch entire seasons of action-filled programs that I've downloaded to my phone from my favorite streaming channels. Time flies on by. And I discovered an added benefit: I actually walk faster because of the action. I only allow myself to watch my shows on the treadmill, so I look forward to returning to the gym the next day to see what happens next. The result upon the writing of this book is that I haven't missed a day since December 2018. Score!

Being physically fit impacts your travel bucket list. As we age, travel needs and considerations change. Consider your physical fitness for bucket list trips and prioritize the more active ones to experience sooner rather than later. One client lamented that they had dreamed of going to Greece for 25 years. When they finally retired and went on the trip, they were not as physically fit as they would have liked to be to enjoy the walking tours, trekking up the Parthenon, and snorkeling the Greek Islands. Revisit the curious list that you completed in chapter three, in addition to your bucket list, and add some physical fitness activities.

> *Laughter is heard with our head but felt with our heart, proof that it comes from the soul.*
>
> *~Judi Snyder*

Lose the Belly, Not the Belly Laugh

How often have we heard the phrase "laughter is the best medicine"? Maybe it never gets old because it is a timeless universal truth. Think about how great you feel after a good belly laugh. Laughter makes us happy. Happiness keeps us healthy. Did you know that research has shown that individuals with a deeper sense of happiness possess lower levels of inflammatory gene responses and higher levels of antiviral gene responses? Yes, laughter increases your immune response. Who couldn't use that in a post-Covid-19 world? Check out an article on the benefits of laughter by Lawrence Robinson, Melinda Smith, M.A., and Jeanne Segal, Ph.D. listed on the www.helpguide. org website.

Laughter relaxes the whole body. A good, hearty laugh relieves physical tension and stress, leaving muscles relaxed for up to 45 minutes afterward.

Laughter boosts the immune system. Laughter decreases stress hormones and increases immune cells and infection-fighting antibodies, thus improving resistance to disease.

Laughter triggers the release of endorphins. Endorphins are the body's natural feel-good chemicals. They promote an overall sense of well-being and can even temporarily relieve pain.

Laughter protects the heart. Laughter improves the function of blood vessels and increases blood flow, which can help protect against heart attack and other cardiovascular problems.

Laughter burns calories. Okay, so it's no replacement for going to the gym, but research has found that laughing for 10 to 15 minutes a day can burn approximately forty calories. That could be enough to lose three or four pounds over the course of a year.

Laughter lightens anger's heavy load. Nothing diffuses anger and conflict faster than a shared laugh. Looking at the funny side can put problems into perspective and enable you to move on from confrontations without holding onto bitterness or resentment.

Laughter may even help you to live longer. A study in Norway found that people with a strong sense of humor outlived those who didn't laugh as much. The difference was particularly notable for those battling cancers.

We love to laugh and hate to worry, yet we spend more time worrying than laughing. Worrying is analogous to praying for what you don't want, so let's become intentional about incorporating more laughing into our daily life. Laughing is a very large part of wellness. It helps our mind, body, and spirit. Laughter can improve relationships, whether with romantic partners, friends and family, or co-workers. In any of these scenarios, you can learn to use laughter as a powerful tool for managing conflict and reducing tension when emotions are running high. Humor lowers your stress levels and induces positive communication so your relationships can move forward instead of spiraling downward. Relationships are foundational in our wellness journey; we will dive deeper into relationships in the next chapter.

Choosersizes – Take a Self-Care Sabbatical

🐚 Examine your diet and list three changes you can make immediately that will positively impact your health.

🐚 Commit to one form of exercise that you can do every day, and an additional one that you can do several times a week.

🐚 Aim to laugh every day.

*Download the companion workbook
www.BecomingRetiredishWorkbook.com

Chapter 5

THE FLAW OF ASSOCIATION

Choose to Be Where You Are Celebrated, Not Tolerated

Are you *shoulding* your relationships? You may think it's odd that social connection is discussed in the wellness section of this book. Social connection is a key ingredient in upsizing your joy and wellness in retirement. Research has proven that our relationships can impact our health as much as or more than diet and exercise. Stressful and draining relationships have a profound effect on our body chemistry. A study by *Berkman Lisa F, Syme Leonard. Social Networks, Host Resistance, and Mortality: A Nine-Year Followup Study of Alameda County Residents,* American Journal of Epidemiology, 1979 showed that the risk of death among men and women with the fewest social ties was more than twice as high as the risk for adults with the most social ties. Moreover, this finding held true even when socioeconomic status, health behaviors, and other variables that might influence mortality were considered.

Relationships have such an impact on our physical and mental health, yet we rarely, if ever, re-evaluate our circle of friends to determine whether we feel full or empty after spending time with them. Your friends and social activities may change over time. After all, we are ever evolving so it makes sense that our relationships may need to evolve along with us. Some relationships start out great but develop into unhealthy, lopsided attachments. Have you ever noticed that some people bring out the best in you and some, well, not so much? You can't have a healthy relationship with an unhealthy person. Just as some foods can be healthy for one person and cause an allergic reaction in another, my belief is that people can also have this effect. This doesn't make them wrong or a bad person, it just means you may have outgrown each other. Taking the time to evaluate your relationships will provide awareness of your motivations for your alliances as well as insight into your behavior.

Recognize that when you become retiredish, work friends may keep in touch less often, or not at all, because you no longer have as much in common with them. Once you leave your company or industry, the topics and activities that interest you naturally change. If you haven't yet retired, notice as you are interacting with your work friends how much of your conversation involves topics outside the work environment. Start to develop a network of friends outside of work, such as through book clubs, card clubs like bridge or euchre, or pickleball leagues. Meet-up.com is a good place to find groups that share common interests.

THE FLAW OF ASSOCIATION

Before we get into the jungle brush of relationships, we need to talk about victimhood, the elephant in the relationship room. Victimhood has no place in any relationship on either side. If you are living at the corner of victimhood and it's-not-my-fault mindset, move out of the 'hood and relocate fast. We all most likely have a friend or two who live in the victim 'hood, the friend things always seem to happen to. I'm not suggesting we abandon every imperfect person in our lives because we are all imperfect. If you notice you are surrounded by people who are victims, then it is time to take a moment and assess who you are spending your time with and why. What are you getting out of those relationships? What are they getting out of their relationship with you? Your actions are the result of your conscious choosing, not habitual default. You are not obligated to continue any relationship just because of the length of time you've been in that relationship.

Rahav Gabay, *The tendency for interpersonal victimhood: The personality construct and its Consequences. 2020 Rahav Gabaya, Boaz Hameirib, Tammy Rubel-Lifschitzd, Arie Nadlera,* define the tendency for interpersonal victimhood as "an ongoing feeling that the self is a victim, which is generalized across many kinds of relationships. As a result, victimization becomes a central part of the individual's identity." Those who have a perpetual victimhood mindset tend to have an external locus of control, believing that life is entirely under the control of forces outside oneself, such as fate or luck, or at the mercy of other people. I believe we have full control and responsibility for our life, that we are 100 percent responsible for ourselves. Everything that we believe happens *to* us, happens *for* us, for our spiritual growth. We can all recount stories of people who have had horrific things happen in their lives and turned around and made something beautiful and world-changing out of the experience. Conversely, we also know people who withdraw after a tragic experience and live the rest of their lives in bitterness and self-destruction. This is *your choice*. At some point you need to unpack those victim bags and relocate from that corner of victimhood and it's-not-my-fault to the boulevard of personal responsibility. This is not an easy choice and there will be a period of necessary mourning from the void. Grief is an essential part of moving through your pain process; not underneath your pain, not around your pain, but *through* your pain. This will take time, be kind to yourself. We grieve all sorts of things—people, friendships, pets, jobs, homes, and dreams. Grief is an indication of how much we've loved. You can never love too much, and love is never a bad thing. Grief recovery is an integral part of joyful living. The age at which we become retiredish is the age when we experience the most loss of loved ones and things loved. For this reason, the next chapter is entirely devoted to processing grief. Understanding the stages of grief will help move us through the process in the healthiest way possible.

If you find that you are not the victim but that many people you have relationships with are, you may be a rescuer and that isn't healthy either. Rescuers need to be needed. Rescuers' self-esteem takes a huge hit when they don't have anyone to rescue. Rescuers attract victims like bees to flowers. It's the perfect union. In a 2011 *Psychology Today* article, *The Rescuer Identity*, Andrea Matthews defines the rescuer as enabling the unconscious encouragement of another's dis-ability. Resentment and anger are usually an indication you are the rescuer in a relationship. If you find your self-talk saying "I don't understand how they could do this or that to me when I've done this or that for them," you might be a rescuer.

THE FLAW OF ASSOCIATION

Rescuing doesn't always appear to be undesirable. The very trait that made you successful in your career could sabotage your personal life. Think about all the accolades you've received in your work. Most of the time, they were earned through your efforts when rescuing the company, an employee, or the boss out of a situation in which your expertise became the salvation. We all want to feel needed and appreciated, but it's important to notice when the need for appreciation crosses the line to make someone a rescuer. This leaves us with quite a quandary. How do we determine whether we are a supportive and caring person or a rescuer?

Cheri Gregory, in her book *The Cure for the "Perfect" Life,* asked this question and observed the following:

1) Helping is providing someone with the tools to succeed. Rescuing is doing it all for them.
2) Helping is assisting someone to do something for themselves. Rescuing is saving someone from the consequences of their actions or the actions of another.
3) Helping is coming alongside another to give advice, support, or resources during a difficult time. Rescuing is taking ownership of another's problem and making it your mission to fix it or them.

As you think about your relationships with others, consider who you are and how you behave when you are with those people. We can act differently with different people. This is your time to reflect and reassess your relationships with others as well as your relationship with yourself.

> You can't have a healthy relationship with an unhealthy person. To be healthy, you must be happy with yourself first.
>
> ~Judi Snyder

Relationship with Your Significant Other

One discovery made by the newly retired is that they find they are no longer as enamored with their spouse or partner when they are together 24/7. Being together all day when you haven't been for years is an opportunity to examine how you want to spend your time together. We may have had a glimpse of this during the Covid-19 lockdown. Failure to prepare for sudden 24/7 togetherness combined with today's increased life expectancy has contributed to the increase in uncoupling. Divorce rates of those over fifty (the recently termed *gray divorce*) has roughly doubled over the last 25 years. Incorporate your spouse or partner into your life before retirement and find activities you enjoy together. Likewise, encourage each other to cultivate friends and activities with others that you don't have to do as a couple. This becomes vitally important if or when one passes away before the other.

Lastly, determine whether you and your partner are extrovert, introvert, omnivert, or ambivert:

- 🐚 **Extrovert**—an outgoing, overtly expressive person who predominantly gains energy by interacting with external stimuli.
- 🐚 **Introvert**—typically quieter and more concerned with their inner life, withdrawing into themselves to recharge their batteries.
- 🐚 **Ambivert**—someone whose overall behavior is a balance between introversion or extroversion.
- 🐚 **Omnivert**—someone who can be either an introvert or an extrovert at different times.

In addition to understanding your basic personality driver, knowing your partner's "love languages" can greatly improve your relationships. Gary Chapman wrote a series of books on the five love languages for romantic relationships, children, workplace, and even for blended families. I highly recommend visiting https://www.5lovelanguages.com/ and reading at least one of Chapman's books to learn the best way to create and nurture the relationships that are important to you.

Now that you have an idea of each other's personality drivers, talk about each other's need for alone time or social time so it is not a surprise to either of you when retirement comes. Revisit your internal spirituality or personal driving values from chapter one. Knowing each other's guiding values and personality drivers helps tremendously when seeking activities and socializing as a retired couple. For example, I'm a flaming extrovert whose number-one value is relationships and I am energized by social connection. My husband, Jeff, is an omnivert (balance of extrovert/introvert) who enjoys socializing but needs alone time to decompress after being around high-energy situations. Knowing our differences means we can plan our activities so we can both nurture and honor our differences. I often plan a trip to spend some quality time with my BFF on the east coast of Florida. This allows Jeff his decompression time and it's a win/win for both of us.

Choices Have Consequences

Remember the values conversation in chapter one? Your internal spiritual drivers are the steering wheel of your behavior. This is a great reminder that not everyone has the same steering wheel. Others may at some point take different roads than the roads you are choosing on your journey. This is neither good nor bad, it just is. Whether it is evaluating your relationship with your spouse/partner or friends circle, you can begin to understand which relationships serve your highest best self by using the Four R's of Relationship Review and completing the "Friends Fitness Choosersize."

Friendships: The 4R's of Relationship Review

1. **RECOGNIZE**

   Recognizing relationships that no longer serve us is perhaps one of the biggest contributors to overall wellness, but it's not that easy. Toxic relationships are not easy to release, but they tend to be easier to spot than relationships that are just "meh," the ones that are not explicitly damaging but no longer serve us and lift us up. We've all had relationships with generally nice people, good people, who for whatever reason we no longer enjoy. We find it a chore to get together, and we don't feel good after being around them. I'll use a food analogy. Which is harder to say no to: appealing and delicious cakes, cookies, and gluten-filled bready carbs with corn syrup and trans hydrogenated fat or a bottle of poison with skull and crossbones? The cakes look and taste heavenly, but can leave us feeling bloated, sugar-crashing after we eat them and wanting more. Nice people who no longer bring us joy can be camouflaged in much the same way. Relationships with nice people we have outgrown is something we rarely think about addressing, but on an energetic level can adversely affect our health.

Some relationships begin positive but can become negative over time because we are all on individual journeys that grow and move in different directions. Many times, relationships that are not reciprocal can end up becoming toxic, so it's best to recognize the signs early on to avoid the drama later. Recognizing people who are not bringing you joy or lifting you up is an exercise that will be worth your time and exponentially increase your joy if you spend some time to evaluate on a regular basis.

You have probably heard the saying. "People are in your life for a reason, a season, or a lifetime." There may be people from your past who you absolutely adored, who had an impact on your life and career, who maybe just brought you joy and laughter. Pick up the phone and connect with them from time to time and let them know how they impacted you. I recently learned that the husband of a friend of mine passed away. Kathy and Dan were friends from years ago, who I had met because we worked together. We lost touch due to career changes and relocations, but that didn't mean that they had any less positive impact on my life. When we were together, we laughed and had loads of fun. I was single at the time and their relationship was an inspiration to me. It had been more than 25 years since I spent time with this couple, but I dearly loved them both and their impact was not diminished because we lost touch. Kathy and I connected, and I was able to express my condolences and gratitude for their friendship, but it would have been so nice to have been able to do that with Dan before he passed. Think about those long-ago relationships that had impact and let them know how they changed your life.

Friendship is as important to the soul as water is to the body. Devote some time to evaluate your circle of friends. Determine who you want to expand or limit your time with so you can surround yourself with those who bring you joy. Begin by completing the "Friend Fitness" choosersize, listing the friends or circle of people you spend the most time with and indicate how you feel when you are with them and after spending time with them. Reflect on past situations when you needed support. Did they support you or your venture? After you have contemplated these areas and determined how you feel around these friends, it is time to categorize them. Do you want to continue the relationship, limit association, or disassociate completely? There are some people who will drop to limited association because they will always be in your life no matter how they make you feel. By default, these people will go in the limited association category. Some difficult family members and ex partners or spouses are usually in this category, especially if you have children together. If you have determined that a person does not make you feel good while you are with them or after you're with them and you have no familial ties that bind you, it is time to lovingly release the relationship. Disassociation, the act of permanently releasing the relationships that no longer serve you, will leave you feeling like a weight has been lifted. A word of caution: Before you start axing your friends, keep it real. All relationships ebb and flow according to what is going on in your life and theirs, but in general, does this person add or subtract from your life energy, are they bringing joy to your life?

The next step is to determine whether you want to increase, decrease, or release the time you spend with your friend list. Deciding how best to do that with integrity, decisiveness, and peace can be tricky because we are not accustomed to using our choose muscles. Using steps two to four will help you determine what needs to happen next.

2. RESET

Reset your goal or expectation. Helicopter up and ask yourself, what am I trying to achieve? The big reset question is, how much do I share with another when I want to let go of that relationship? You must be willing to accept the consequences of resetting the relationship and the risk that the other person may not respond as you anticipated. Is hurting someone by being unnecessarily mean going to serve anyone? Do you want an enemy, or would you prefer the relationship to just drift away? How can you mindfully make decisions that honor your internal integrity without hurting another person? Most of the time, breaking up a long-lasting relationship will hurt no matter what either of you says or does; expect that and be willing to accept the consequences.

3. **RESPONSIBILITY**

Blame is a common theme when evaluating whether a relationship is reciprocal or one sided. When you hear your self-talk saying someone should have acted this way or said this or that, it is an indication that you are blaming them for your feelings. Eleanor Roosevelt said, "No one can make you feel inferior without your consent." We cannot blame another for their choice, and we cannot blame ourselves for choosing ourselves first. This is not being selfish or self-serving; it is self-preservation. Preserving your integrity is healthy and best for everyone involved.

Rationalization is a subtle form of blame. Making excuses for why you acted a certain way or looking at what you think someone should have done is blame. Instead, look at the *should* as a gift of clarity that helps you decide to choose you. Sometimes it is human nature to make another person wrong so we can rationalize our gut feelings or make it okay to walk away. Those people aren't wrong; in fact, they made a choice that was best for them at that moment. They may have made the choice consciously or subconsciously and they may or may not accept the consequences of that choice, but it was their choice; it really has little to do with you. English actor and filmmaker Gary Oldman said it best when he coined the phrase, "What people think of me is none of my business!"

When looking back at tough situations, remember all the times you realized that something went against your gut? Your only allegiance is to yourself, your higher self. If we act out of personal integrity, we are doing good for everyone involved. Sometimes we never examine our lives until things begin to fall apart. If you are releasing relationships with integrity and respect, lovingly separating from them is for your highest best self and theirs. You are helping their growth on some level as well as honoring your personal integrity. The saying "a reason, a season or a lifetime" holds true, so understand that the season for this relationship has ended.

4. RELEASE

Release any guilt! You are no more responsible for other people's feelings than they are for yours. Guilt comes from believing we have misbehaved in some way that caused someone else's pain. The truth is, sometimes that is true. We are fallible human beings who make mistakes. Own up to your mistakes, apologize with sincerity, learn from it, and then move on. We are the only living creature who continue to live in the past and beat ourselves up for our missteps. Let us take a lesson from our fur babies—they don't mope around all day because they had an accident on the carpet when they were a puppy, so neither should we. Choosing to forgive your past and move forward is the best thing you can do for both of you. Having an inauthentic relationship is not serving either of you.

A great exercise when evaluating your relationships and how to categorize them is to pray or meditate on each scenario and imagine the "what ifs." Your gut will alert you to the correct path. Sometimes writing gives clarity; journal the "what ifs." Consider the consequences of each "what if," choose a path, accept the results, and move on.

Some people will never like you because your spirit irritates their demons."
~Denzel Washington

Choosersizes – Listen to What is Not Being Said and Say What is Being Felt

🐚 Complete your "Friend Fitness" list, determine how you feel around these friends, and categorize them. Do you want to keep them as friends, limit association, or disassociate completely? How do you perceive your relationship with them? Is one of you a victim? Or both of you? Are you a helper or a rescuer?

🐚 If you have a partner, have you discussed whether you are an extrovert, introvert, omnivert, or ambivert? Have you discussed your love language? Have you planned activities accordingly?

🐚 Pick up the phone occasionally and have an actual conversation with someone who had a positive impact on your life.

*Download the companion workbook
www.BecomingRetiredishWorkbook.com

Chapter 6

GOOD GRIEF!

Grief feels horrible—and it is horrible—but how we move through grief can make a world of difference for our mental and physical health. As you may recall, in chapter five I explained why grief is in the wellness section of a retirement book. Nothing can cut us off at the knees quite like a grief situation, and there is no other time in our lifespan when we are faced with more types of grief than in our "third age" or traditional retirement years. Most of us have lost loved ones, grandparents, parents, friends, animals. We have become empty nesters as our kids became adults, downsized our living space, and ended a career. As we began this book with *Who am I?* in chapter one, most of us discovered that our identities are determined by who we are to others and what we do for a living. Then *boom*, suddenly it's gone. For some folks this can be a seamless transition but for others, grief can preoccupy every waking moment. Whatever the reason you are grieving, the steps to joy and the new normal are the same.

The truth is, no one wants their loved ones to suffer. We all know that upon someone's departure from this world there will be grief. If we've loved, we can't avoid going through grief. Grief is inevitable, so I want to spend some time on grief because we are entering the season of our life cycle where we will have to deal with grief more than we ever have before. Grief can come from many things, the most obvious being the loss of a loved one or pet. Grief can also result from losing your identity after forty years of your working life, losing children to adulthood or the empty nest syndrome, or even losing a dream due to financial or physical limitations. Expecting grief and learning how to move through our grief is important, especially as we age.

Most people want to minimize grief for their loved ones as much as possible. The best way to do that is to make decisions ahead of time that may be difficult for those you love, meaning your loved ones won't have to make those decisions in times of intense crisis and mourning. According to Dr. Janel Phillips, Ph.D., a neuropsychologist at The Henry Ford Health System, *How Coping With Grief Can Affect Your Brain*, most people will experience "grief brain" during and after the loss of a loved one. Grief brain can impact all our emotional and mental functions, including areas within the limbic system and pre-frontal cortex. These involve emotional regulation, memory, multi-tasking, organization, and learning. When these circumstances converge, brain function takes a hit. Phillips goes on to say that if you're overwhelmed with grief, it stands to reason that you won't absorb your environment the same way you would when you are content. By making important decisions before your departure to the heavens, you are giving the greatest parting gift to your loved ones: the gift of not requiring them to make emotional, potentially permanent, and regretful decisions while in a state of temporary cognitive impairment.

Understanding the Stages of Grief

Many of us who have gone through grief have heard an insensitive person mutter "just get over it" or "move on." Grief isn't something to skip over. Grief must be felt, fully and consciously, so you can begin to heal. Think of it as an operation. If someone breaks an ankle and it requires surgery, like yours truly did in 2000, it freakin' hurt like heck. First came the pain and shock of the initial break. Then came the surgery, with more nuts and bolts than the aisles of Home Depot. Once the surgery was over, my pain changed from acute to intermittent and then finally subsided, but my ankle was altered forever. I had to rehabilitate my ankle with physical therapy, which was a new and different kind of pain, more of an ache. Then, finally, the healing, the new normal. My ankle was pain free, but forever gone were the days of three-inch heels. I had to adjust to my new normal footwear. Grief is much the same when it attacks our mental health. We must expect the pain, honor the pain, and learn to focus on what we have gained from the person or thing we are grieving.

In 1969, Elisabeth Kübler-Ross identified and wrote about the five stages of grief: denial, anger, bargaining, depression, and acceptance. Recognizing and understanding each stage helps us learn how to live without the one we lost or the thing we grieve. The process is not linear and there is no definitive time to move through this process. We can and will pass back and forth through these stages as we process our emotions.

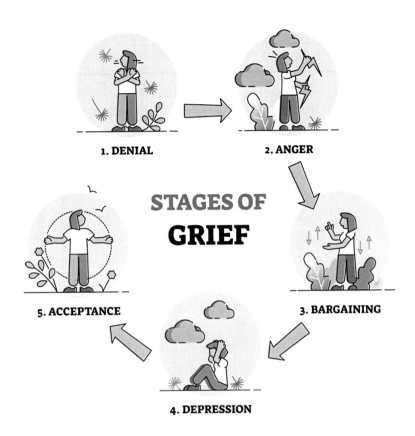

STAGES OF GRIEF

1. DENIAL
2. ANGER
3. BARGAINING
4. DEPRESSION
5. ACCEPTANCE

Denial

Denial initially helps us survive loss. Life doesn't make sense and it can be overwhelming. Your life as you knew it will never be the same. Even when you expect death due to terminal illness you will still experience a state of denial, but it may look different. For example, when my mom, at the age of fifty-three, was diagnosed with terminal brain cancer I was in denial. Even though my career at the time was in the sales and marketing of diagnostic imaging equipment and I made a living looking at brain tumor images, I just couldn't believe that my mom had this diagnosis. I convinced myself it was a mistake because she was diagnosed at a small hospital in my little town in northeastern Pennsylvania and they didn't have the proper up-to-date equipment. My focused and determined self quickly had her transported to Philadelphia where there was a plethora of leading-edge teaching hospitals equipped with the most current equipment used in research not yet available to the general public. I was on it, there must be some error. I convinced myself of this for days until my family, along with my beloved mom, were sitting in a neuro-intensive care unit two days later on New Year's Eve. I heard three words from the distinguished doctor that would completely change my life: "Maybe six weeks." Enter denial again. No, not my mom. I convinced myself that there must be a reason this was happening to me. It was because I had access to the latest and greatest of physicians and technology and my mom would be the first person ever to survive this disease. The truth is, I needed this denial to survive instead of completely falling apart.

Anger

Once reality sets in, anger arrives. You begin the never-ending questioning. Why me? Life's not fair! You might redirect your anger toward close friends and family. You might start to question your belief in God. You might feel you are being punished for something. Researchers and mental health professionals agree that anger is a necessary stage of grief. Encourage the anger. It's important to truly feel it instead of suppressing it. Even though it might seem as though you are in an endless cycle of anger, it will dissipate. The more you truly feel the anger, the more quickly it will dissipate, and the more quickly you will heal. It is not healthy to suppress your feelings of anger. When you suppress your anger inward, that is called depression. Depression is harder to move through because it is fed by an endless loop of unproductive internal self-talk that spirals downward. In my case, I began to get angry at people I didn't know, like the homeless person smoking a cigarette on the corner. I'd ask why my mom had to die from cancer when she was relentless in living a healthy lifestyle. My mom was ahead of her time with healthy eating and regular exercise, whereas there are so many people abusing their bodies. I became judgmental, and I mean ugly judgmental. I became depressed, my physical health suffered, and I gained a ton of weight because I was eating like crap and had no energy to exercise. I told myself it didn't matter. Look what had happened to my healthy mom. Had it not been for some very good BFFs in my life, I don't know where I would have ended up. You will go down this road. When you begin to feel yourself going through this stage, ask for help. People who love you want to support you and will be by your side as you process your feelings.

Bargaining

The "making deals" stage is called bargaining. It goes something like this: Please God, if you <fill in the blank>, I will <fill in the blank>. I will never ask another favor and never complain again." You try to avoid the grief through negotiation. If you change this, I'll change that. You are so desperate to get your life back to how it was before the grief event, you are willing to make a major life change in an attempt toward normalcy. Guilt is the common wingman of bargaining. This is when you endure the never-ending "if only" and "what if" statements. What if I had left the house five minutes sooner—the accident would never have happened. If only I had noticed the symptoms sooner. In my case, I asked myself what would have happened if I had noticed my mom's headaches sooner and encouraged her to go to the doctor six months earlier. The cancer could have been found at an earlier stage and she would still be alive. I should have known, because I was in the field and had more information than most. Another endless loop of unproductive self-talk. This is the time for a good self-check question. Ask yourself this: If someone you love were engaging in the "what if" spiral, would you tell them, "You're right, it's your fault" Would you blame them? I didn't think so. Then why would you blame yourself?

Depression and Anxiety

When anger isn't productively dealt with, depression rears its ugly head. Depression is a commonly accepted form of grief. In fact, most people immediately associate depression with grief—as it is a "present" emotion. It highlights our emptiness and forces our new normal into being. In this stage, you might withdraw from life, feel numb, live in a fog, and not want to get out of bed. The world might seem too much and too overwhelming for you to face. You don't want to be around others, you don't feel like talking, and you experience feelings of hopelessness. You might even experience suicidal thoughts—thinking "what's the point of carrying on?" Anxiety is also part of the equation. Another way of dealing with depression is over-functioning or by becoming a workaholic. Controlling behavior and becoming overly responsible for your family and friends or work is an anxiety response. You are compensating for the lack of control over your loss. Recognizing over-functioning can be difficult. Some examples of manifestation include becoming obsessed with scheduling, constantly reminding people of things, micro-managing, and giving unsolicited advice. If you find yourself insisting on always planning the trips or choosing the restaurants in which you socialize it might be a good indication you are over-functioning.

How do you tell the difference between over-functioning and just plain old "driver" personality, which is a positive attribute? The biggest difference is having a team around you and including others in the decision. It's one thing to be the organizer (driver) and another to make the decisions without input (over-functioning). It is sometimes hard to distinguish between the two, especially in the early stages. I'm your classic first-born natural driver personality. When my driver attribute morphed into over-functioning as my grief response, it was years before I noticed. I started to notice that I was making excuses for making decisions without other people's input: I don't want to bother them; they can't get the same deal I can get; I can fix this faster than it would take to discuss it. These are just a few examples of my self-talk.

Resentment and feeling personally responsible are good indicators you have crossed the line. Notice whether you are the one who ends up "making it rain" all the time. Although you get a temporary bump in self-esteem, over the long haul it leaves you feeling empty and resentful. When you find that you are making decisions in a bubble and feeling a bit resentful, it's time to reflect. Journal to understand your triggers. Once you become aware of them, you can't un-see them!

Acceptance

The last stage of grief identified by Kübler-Ross is acceptance (not in the sense that "it's okay," but knowing that you will be okay). You've come to terms with your new reality. You are learning to live with the grief, and it has become integrated in a healthy way into your new life. You learn to appreciate life's experiences—holidays, births, weddings, and sad songs—in a new way. You may finally be earning a living doing something you've always wanted to do but didn't previously allow yourself to explore. You realize that your loved one lives in your heart, and you begin to notice signs that they are still with you, guiding you and loving you.

As difficult as it can be to initiate a conversation about life after death with someone who is dying, I implore you to have that conversation. We are afraid because we don't want our loved one to think that we don't believe they can conquer a disease or that we have given up. Do it before someone becomes ill or passes suddenly from an unfortunate accident or untimely death. I am most grateful for conversations I had with my mother before she passed away and I consider them a blessing from the time we spent together during her terminal illness. We would talk endlessly about what her signs would be from heaven and how I would recognize them. We joked and cried and in the end, she gave me specific signs. Seeing those signs after she passed has given me comfort beyond words.

You will move in and out of these stages throughout your grief and throughout the years. Every time someone passes it may reignite these feelings in one way or another. However, you will eventually notice that there will come a time when you are mostly in acceptance, and this is completely normal. When you can finally see the "blessings in the messings" you have probably arrived at acceptance.

Symptoms of Grief

It is important to recognize the symptoms so you can begin honoring the process of grieving. Your grief symptoms may present themselves physically, socially, or spiritually. Some of the most common symptoms of grief are presented below:

- Tears
- Headaches
- Difficulty sleeping
- Questioning the purpose of life
- Questioning your spiritual beliefs (e.g., your belief in God)
- Feelings of detachment
- Isolation from friends and family
- Abnormal behavior
- Worry
- Anxiety
- Frustration
- Guilt
- Fatigue
- Anger
- Loss of appetite
- Aches and pains
- Stress

Things to Know Before You Go

The survey asked one simple question: What gives you peace of mind? The number one answer: I want to know my loved ones will be taken care of. I was shocked the answer wasn't about money. Working in financial services, I most often hear people express fear about running out of money in retirement. Although that is certainly a major concern, it takes a back seat to knowing their loved ones will be fine. So what, exactly, does "taken care of" mean? The statement is ambiguous and could mean a whole host of things, from leaving your loved ones a legacy of money, vacation homes, or family heirlooms to passing on your familial values. Peace of mind can be like the last stage of grief: acceptance, that feeling of, "I'm okay, I have no regrets." However, there are a few areas that can bubble up over and over, interfere with peace of mind, and prevent you from entering the "no regrets" zone.

Forgiveness is the Best Rewind

Lack of forgiveness is the most prevalent and emotional inhibitor of peace of mind, by far. Remembering something I had heard (I wish life had a rewind button), I asked another simple question: What is your number one rewind moment? Most all the answers I received were about forgiveness and conversations that never happened. Sometimes the forgiveness rewind was not about forgiving another person, but rather about forgiving ourselves for past mistakes. Forgiving ourselves is *the* most difficult of all. If you are unable to forgive yourself, you will not be able to fully forgive others. Forgiveness is a choice. Forgiveness requires empathy, compassion, kindness, and understanding. The best way to forgive yourself for anything is to reframe the mistake. I suggest three steps, the triple A's, to reframe mistakes and create your forgiveness rewind:

1. **Adopt** the philosophy that things happen *for* me, not *to* me. Mistakes are about detours. You wouldn't hold a grudge the rest of your life for making a wrong turn on a road trip, so why are you doing this with your life's decisions? Sometimes these detours help you discover the unknown beauty you would have otherwise missed with monocular vision. Looking for the gold in any mistake is essential to moving through the process of forgiving. Rarely do we get anything right the first time. Innovation and invention are born out of mistakes. America was discovered by a ship being only degrees off course. Embrace the detours with curiosity and as a nudge to change course and look for the gold.

2. **Address** your self-talk as though you were teaching a small child you love. I'm willing to bet you wouldn't speak to a child the way you speak to yourself. A great way to practice positive inner-speak is to take a picture of your five-year-old self and have an out-loud conversation about the mistake and how or what might have been learned from it. Take your own time-out to reflect on how to move forward. Most everyone is compassionate with children; we are harshest with our ourselves. This exercise helps tame our inner critic and gives us the space and permission to reframe the experience.

3. **Acknowledge** the gold that was born from the mistake. Look back and review what you may have missed had you *not* made the mistake. Many people look back negatively at a bad marriage, yet rarely acknowledge the blessing of the children that came from that marriage. Some mistakes aren't so obvious, but there is always gold in every mishap.

Embracing the Yuck

Forgiving others is not easy by any means, but we are able to forgive others more easily than we forgive ourselves. To forgive those who hurt you can significantly improve both psychological wellbeing and physical health. Forgiveness is not about forgiving an act against us or excusing the person who committed the act. Forgiveness is about acknowledging that person as a fallible human being who made a mistake because something inside of them was wounded. It is not about you. Let me repeat, *it is not about you.* Hurt people hurt people. By forgiving others, you break the cycle. Anger causes stress, and prolonged stress can lead to heart disease among other health ailments. In a 2016 study *Forgiveness, Stress, and Health: a 5-Week Dynamic Parallel Process Study*, Loren L. Toussaint found that when forgiveness rose, stress levels went down. Reduced stress, in turn, led to a decrease in negative mental health and physical symptoms.

If you are old enough to be retiredish, then chances are you've harbored a grudge or two in your life. I know I have. Here is the good news for grudge holders: We can learn to forgive. That's right, forgiveness is a learned behavior. The first step toward forgiveness is to have empathy for the person you want to forgive. We can use the "Triple A" approach with others just as we used it for our self. We can adopt a simple philosophy: If someone is doing something to us, then there is something we can learn from this event. We can look at that person with compassion and recognize that their inner child has been wounded; usually, in hindsight, we can see some gift that arose from being hurt by that person. If we practice with strangers, we can get better when we want to forgive those closest to us. We've all had experiences with customer service people who seem more like the sales prevention department than customer service, or we may have experienced a curt restaurant server. Their attitude toward us rarely has anything to do with us personally. They may be having a bad day, or they just may be an unhappy person, but it is not about us. If we practice with small situations, then the bigger situations become easier.

The Japanese believe that embracing the cracks or damages makes something more beautiful. This is an art form called *kintsukuroi*. They believe that imperfections are to be celebrated; once something broken is mended, it is stronger for having gone through the break and it possesses a unique character that can never be duplicated. Forgiveness is a muscle that needs to be exercised. Just as with working any other muscle, you can't expect to be buff overnight. Forgive the small things before the ginormous things. Be patient and compassionate with yourself in this process. If forgiveness were easy, there would be no war. It is not easy, but it is necessary for happiness and well-being.

Spiritual Discussion

"Things left unsaid and the courage to express my feelings" is one of the top five regrets lamented by the dying. Difficult conversations are, well, difficult. It is difficult to have a conversation about dying with a person battling cancer or a parent in their eighties. It is difficult to speak of death when someone is fighting for their life. It is the unknown that makes us uncomfortable to approach the subject, since we have no experience to speak of. We like to stick to what we think we know. Difficult conversations about the spiritual hereafter are riddled with unknowns. We tell ourselves, "Someday we'll get around to having that death conversation," but that day never comes. There is a plethora of research proving that people would rather stay in a horrific and abusive situation because it is familiar, rather than facing the unknown. If you knew with certainty that having those difficult conversations about the unknown would bring you and those you love peace of mind, would you consider the discussion?

From the *Journal of Palliative Medicine, February 2000, Taking a Spiritual History Allows Clinicians to Understand Patients More Fully,*

GOOD GRIEF!

Dr. Christina Puchalski developed a tool for spiritual discussion to better identify the spiritual needs of patients, and I recommend we use the same tool for our discussions with loved ones. By having spiritual discussion, you gift your loved ones with the permission to discuss issues of importance to them without judgment. Puchalski uses an acronym, FICA (faith, importance, community, address). I've included her model and summarized it as follows:

> **F** represents *Faith*—Do you consider yourself religious or spiritual? Do you have faith or a belief in a higher power? What gives meaning to your life? Do you believe in life after death, reincarnation, resurrection?
>
> **I** represents *Importance*—Is your spiritual belief important in your life? How do you want to integrate your belief into the memory of your loved ones?
>
> **C** represents *Community*—Are you part of a spiritual or faith community? How do you want to be remembered by that community and who do you want to participate in memorial services? Do you want burial or cremation?
>
> **A** represents *Address*—How can your loved ones and healthcare providers address and respect your wishes in the care and handling of your affairs before and after you pass?

Spirituality is an important, if not essential, component of each person's overall well-being. Spirituality is a dynamic and ongoing issue; readdress it over time. As we age, we tend to focus on our spirituality more. Keep in mind this is about your loved one and be cautious not impose your beliefs onto others. Conversations with loved ones about death are difficult, but I promise they will be comforting and healing when someone passes. As I shared when we were learning about grief, I experienced this opportunity when my beloved mother was dying of brain cancer. I now consider it to be one of my greatest blessings. We would talk for hours about life after death. We even joked at times about what her "sign" would be, a sign that would allow me to know unequivocally that she was with me in spirit. She passed in 1992 at the too-young age of fifty-three, and those conversations have healed me immensely, beyond expectation, over these years. I have peace of mind knowing there was nothing left unsaid and her wishes were carried out. I continue to appreciate our predetermined signs that pop up on a regular basis to remind me she is with me, guides me, and lives on in my heart. You don't want your loved ones ruminating about the mind-numbing "what ifs" and "maybes." Having these difficult conversations will allow you to revel in the delight of your happy memories and heal. You may even consider making videos and writing a book so your "soul legacy" can be passed on for generations to come.

Money Matters

We will delve into the financial element more deeply in the next section, but while we are on the subject of "things to know before you go" and "no regrets," a few things are worth mentioning now. First, if you have a spouse or partner and you are living a lifestyle that requires both incomes, both of you should have a plan to replace your income. The loss of one of those incomes can be catastrophic for the partner left behind. You don't want your loved one having to worry about survival during their time of grief. Second, have a plan for long-term care because no plan is still a plan. You don't want to have to rely on family, friends, or the government. And third, depending on the size and structure of your estate, you may need a more comprehensive estate plan that would include trusts. If you determine you need to include trusts in your estate plan, please consider the following two biggest errors we see in our practice:

1. Spending beaucoup bucks on attorneys to set up a trust and then never funding it or retitling assets in the trust's name.

2. Failing to discuss the terms of the trust with the beneficiaries. Many times, the trustee becomes the bad guy or gal when they withhold money from the beneficiaries because they are obligated to follow the trust documents. Having the conversation prior to your passing can help make the process easier and may even help with additional ideas.

B.Y.E. List, Love in Action

As a retirement and transition consultant, I am often called when someone passes on to assist in end-of-life matters. Whether a person's passing is anticipated or the result of an unexpected illness or accident, the shock is just as earth shattering. Regardless of the reason for the passing of a loved one—anticipated illness, suicide, sudden illness, or accident—there is a gamut of emotions that interfere with a person's ability to focus and rationally deal with the burial and closing of the estate. The emotions range from guilt to relief that your loved one is no longer suffering, from anger or shock, and many times from a combination of all of these. Having a "brain trust" or financial team in place, and having your personal papers and documents organized, is one of the best gifts you can give your loved ones at a time when they are least able to make solid decisions. Remember the "grief brain" from earlier? It kicks in fast and furiously.

Not so fun fact from Women's Institute for a Secure Retirement ...

80% of men die married.
80% of women die single.
Whether you are a man or a woman, have a well-thought-out plan for what will happen with your assets in either scenario.

At the end of this chapter, a Choosersize will require you to complete what I call your B.Y.E. List (an acronym for Before You Exit). I consider the B.Y.E. List to be love in action; completing this list when you are alive will provide your loved ones with the greatest of gifts: peace of mind. As you read through this section, you can begin gathering the information to complete your B.Y.E. List.

Everyone needs a team to support them throughout life. You probably have one but might not have all their information in one place. Develop your "brain trust" team and make a list that includes contact info for everyone—best phone numbers, addresses, and emails. The team may include an estate planning attorney, insurance agents, financial advisors, CPAs/accounting professionals, bankers, cryptocurrency accounts, and other financial institutions. Be sure to have this list at the top of the file. Designate a known location such as a filing cabinet, safe, or safety deposit box, and discuss this file with several people you trust. At the end of this chapter, I will introduce two web-based/app applications you can utilize to guide you through this process.

GOOD GRIEF!

Next, you will want to organize your important documents so they are easily accessed by your loved ones when they want to discuss things with your brain trust team. I recommend organizing these documents in the following four categories:

1. Estate Planning
2. Insurance
3. Investments
4. Personal

If you have not yet done your estate planning, please consider making this a priority. Many people have the misconception that if they don't have a lot of money, they do not need an estate plan. Having a plan protects you from others making decisions you don't agree with regarding your end-of-life wishes or the estate you worked hard to build during your life. I cannot stress enough how difficult it becomes for your loved ones to unanimously make tough decisions about your end-of-life wishes. Many times, families are torn apart by the difference in interpretation of your wishes. Make your desires clear and have the discussion with everyone in attendance. Your estate planning file may include documents such as:

a. Medical advance directive
b. Living will
c. Durable and financial power of attorney
d. Healthcare proxy
e. Pre-paid burial account
f. Information for obituary

Be sure your beneficiaries are up to date on all your insurance products and be sure to include secondary beneficiaries in the event your primary beneficiary predeceases you. Understand the difference between **per stirpes** and **per capita** when designating your beneficiaries. Let's consider an example with two children listed as the primary beneficiaries. Per capita typically means an equal distribution among your living children; if one child predeceases you, the entire asset goes to the remaining living child. With per stirpes, the living child receives half and the children of the deceased child get the other half.

Your insurance file may include documents such as:

    a. Life insurance policies
    b. Long-term care policies
    c. Annuities
    d. Home and vehicle insurance

Investments can be confusing on a good day, even more so when you are mired in grief. There are endless ways to invest your money and endless professionals who offer investments and advice. You may have more than one investment advisor or financial professional on your team. You will want to label each investment with the advisor's contact information specific to that investment so your loved ones are not contacting the incorrect custodian. This could result in letting fees accrue or lapse, or having proceed checks mailed to incorrect addresses. Again, just as with insurance, be sure your beneficiaries are up to date on all your investment products. Your investments file may include documents such as:

a. Brokerage accounts
b. Self-directed investment accounts
c. Online security accounts
d. Investment clubs
e. Stock certificates
f. Bonds
g. Alternative investments (oil and gas, real estate, precious metals), promissory notes
h. Pension plan
i. Profit sharing and purchase plan documents
j. Retirement plans (including 401k, 403b, 457, IRA, SEP IRA, and Roth IRA)
k. Bank records, safe deposit information and keys, and CDs (Certificate of Deposit)
l. Cryptocurrency accounts with secure passwords

"Personal" is likely where everything else will be filed. Your personal file should be updated on a regular basis and should act as your "working" file that is utilized daily. Your personal file may include information such as:

a. Social Security information
b. Home property and vehicle deeds
c. Tax records
d. Military records
e. Passwords to devices and online accounts including cryptocurrency, social media apps, computers, tablets, and cellphone
f. Safe combination and keys
g. Passports and a copy of your driver's license
h. Credit card information
i. Jewelry, collectibles, and other valuables receipts and records
j. Anything else you deem important

Dealing with Debt

Debt is hard to deal with when you are alive and it can be even more overwhelming for your loved ones when you are gone. I see 90 percent of confusion arising from these two areas: the closing of credit card accounts and the closing of an estate and debt repayment for the deceased. There are a couple of areas I want to highlight.

1) **Closing of Credit Cards**

   Most people frantically close out their loved ones' credit cards without the knowledge that in many cases only the person whose Social Security number was used to obtain the credit is responsible for any balance owed on that credit card. Even if you are an authorized user of the credit card, if your credit was not used to obtain the credit line, you might not be required to pay the balance, unless you are in a "joint or community property" state. Depending on your state dollar limits, the creditors may file a lien against the estate and require probate. Most don't bother if the estate is under a specified amount, which varies state by state. I've seen far too many newly widowed clients put themselves in debt by paying a credit card they are not responsible for at a time when half or sometimes three-quarters of their income has terminated. I recommend reviewing each credit card you own for which you have designated an authorized user. Determine whose credit was used to obtain that credit card and note that on the folder in which you file your statements. This will make the process of closing them out go smoothly for your loved ones and it can make all the difference in the world to their financial situation.

2) Closing of an Estate and Debt Repayment

The closing of an estate can be daunting for your loved ones. Having a conversation about your debt prior to your passing can help mitigate or eliminate estate debt in advance. Depending on the amount of debt, strongly consider seeking legal help to resolve an insolvent estate, since there are several legal statutes governing who should be paid and how much. According to www.debt.org, details vary by state. In general, only after arranging to resolve all debts can you distribute assets to heirs. An estate must pay debts in the following order of priority:

- Funeral expenses
- Estate administration costs
- Taxes
- Other general debts; this can be vague and may need legal expertise

If the estate owes more than it is worth, it is considered insolvent. When an estate is insolvent (or near insolvent), negotiation for debt forgiveness is very common. Debtholders may end up with nothing if they don't agree to a lesser amount.

Debt Forgiveness

It is common for some debts to be completely or partially forgiven after death, especially if creditors believe that the estate may not have enough money to pay all debts. If creditor A doesn't agree to forgive some of the debt, the other creditors will be paid first and there may not be enough money left at the end to pay to anything to creditor A. When some or all a debt is forgiven, that means that the person to whom the money was owed has agreed to reduce the size of the debt. You should get any such agreements in writing. You should also be aware that the amount forgiven is considered taxable income for the estate, and that big corporations such as credit card companies will almost certainly report these amounts to the IRS. Of course, few creditors are going to volunteer to forgive their amounts, so you will need to negotiate with them if you wish to get anything reduced. If you have hired a probate attorney, this may be something you delegate to them, since they're familiar with it.

According to www.estateexec.com, the list of exempt assets varies by state, but two major assets are exempt everywhere: retirement savings and life insurance policies. Those two assets can be distributed to beneficiaries without regard to debts owed by the deceased. Some states also designate other entities as exempt, so it's wise to check the laws where you live. Florida, for example, says the surviving spouse or children have the right to exempt household furniture and appliances up to a value of $10,000 as well as two automobiles. Assets that are non-exempt, meaning available to be liquidated and used to pay off debts, would include a house, car, boat, bank account, artwork, stamp or coin collection, and anything that has enough value to be sold.

This table outlines the top 10 most populous state's laws concerning estates that are able to avoid the probate process altogether, or avoid the part of the probate process:

State	Maximum Value of the Estate to Avoid Probate	How Total Estate Value Is Calculated.
California	$166,250 or less	Calculated by adding the total amount of the decedent's personal and real property. See California Probate Code Section 13100.
Texas	$75,000 or less	Calculated by totaling the value of decedent's personal property, not includ[ing] homestead or exempt property. See Texas Estates Code Chapter 205.
Florida	Allows for Summary Administration of Estates valued at $75,000 or less; OR Where decedent has been dead for more than 2 years.	Total estate does not include value of real estate. See Florida Probate Cod[e] 735.201.

York	$50,000 or less	Real estate and property set aside for decedent's family survivors are not counted into the estate's gross value.
~sylvania	$50,000 or less	Total does not include real estate, exempt property, or amounts used for funeral expenses. See Section 3102 of the Pennsylvania Probate, Estates, and Fiduciaries Code.
~s	$100,000 or less	Probate assets do not, and must not, include real estate. See 755 Illinois Compiled Statutes Article XXV Small Estates.
	$35,000 or less OR $100,000 or less and the entire estate transfers to the surviving spouse.	Total does not include jointly owned property, or other exempt probate assets. See Ohio Revised Code 2113.03.
~gia	No full probate required if: (1) no will; (2) no debts owed; AND (3) property is not contested by heirs who agreed upon how it will be distributed.	All heirs must agree on how estate property is to be divided.
Carolina	Personal property $20,000 or less; OR $30,000 or less, if sole surviving spouse as heir is left (skip probate); OR If the surviving spouse inherits the entire estate (simplified probate process).	Total value does not include jointly owned real estate, or other exempt probate assets. See North Carolina General Statutes Chapter 28A-25-1.
~gan	$15,000 or less	No real estate may be included. Total value does not include jointly owned property, or other exempt probate assets. See Michigan Compiled Laws Section 700.3983.

*https://www.legalmatch.com/law-library/article/how-probate-works-a-state-comparison.html

Web-based and Phone Apps to Help You Through the Organizing Process

I appreciate technology when it can help me through tedious and intimidating processes. Here are two applications that I love, available on the cloud and/or mobile phones, that can significantly streamline the process of being organized before and after losing a loved one.

The first application, **Life Exec**®, helps you organize your important documents in an online vault. LifeExec® provides a secure life management web application designed for storing your important information along with tailor-made plans to keep your closest contacts informed during any life event. Life Exec® has a full library of training videos to help you get started. For more information visit: https://lifeexec.com/

The second application, which provides guidance and support for the weeks and months ahead *after* losing a loved one, is called the **Empathy** app. Empathy was created by a team of software developers, estate lawyers, designers, and grief experts who came together with the goal of helping you and your family better cope with the many aspects of loss. For more information visit: https://www.empathy.com/

We can all agree that no one escapes this world alive. When the inevitable arrives, who is best positioned to make those final decisions concerning your legacy? *You!* By addressing these three most important areas, you will be giving your loved ones, and yourself, the ultimate parting gift—peace of mind.

Choosersizes – Regret is More Terrifying Than Change

- 🐚 Complete your Rewind List
- 🐚 Complete your Love in Action B.Y.E. List
- 🐚 Complete the Debt Worksheet in the workbook to identify your debt and develop a plan to eliminate it.

***Download the companion workbook
www.BecomingRetiredishWorkbook.com**

CHOOSING
NANCIAL FREEDOM

"When we are in our working life and get a paycheck every two weeks, we want time reedom.

When we retire and no longer must work, ve want financial certainty. Perhaps all long, we just wanted peace of mind."

~Judi Snyder

Chapter 7

MINDFUL MONEY

A *New York Post* survey polled 2,000 people and more than half said they were not comfortable talking to someone else about their personal finances. Among some of the things people would rather do than talk about their money:

- 68 percent said they would rather talk about their weight than their money.
- 26 percent would rather talk politics with someone they disagree with than write out a financial plan with a family member.
- 16 percent would rather sit through an intense sex scene in a movie with their parents than tell them their biggest financial blunder. Yikes!

According to a CNBC and Acorns' *"Invest in You" Savings Survey,* only 17 percent of respondents said they use a financial advisor.

We are not going to reveal our weight or talk politics, and definitely no steamy sex talk here, but we will begin the discussion about money so you can get comfortable and make mindful decisions. If you haven't exercised the "mindful money" discussion muscles up until now, you are probably going to get fidgety with this section. Pull off the band-aid and let's get going so you can enjoy your retiredish years!

Are You Still Going to a Pediatrician?

I didn't think so. When you were a child, you most likely went to a pediatrician for medical advice on your health and well-being. But I highly doubt you still go to a pediatrician today. You're most likely seeing an internal medicine doctor, or even a doctor specializing in geriatrics. You may also be consulting a specialist for specific medical issues, challenges, or goals. This doesn't mean that the pediatrician you consulted as a child is a bad doctor. They just may not be the best source of medical advice at this point in your physical life cycle.

The same principle is true for your financial advice. As you progress through your financial life cycle, your circumstances, concerns, and goals will change. The advisors you've consulted with previously, at a different place in your financial life cycle, may not have the experience, expertise, or tools necessary to provide guidance at this point and going forward. As with your pediatrician, this doesn't make your current advisors bad. It just means they may not be the best source of financial advice for this portion of your financial life. The financial life cycle comprises two phases: the growth phase and the distribution phase. Most traditional advisors focus on the growth phase of your money. This isn't meant to assume your current advisor, or their firm, doesn't have the expertise to advise you during this phase of your financial life cycle. But it does mean that a different conversation needs to take place to ensure you are meeting the money distribution challenges of your new retiredish life. Engage your current advisor in a discussion concerning their experience with strategies for income distribution. You may want to interview other potential advisors who specialize in this phase of your financial life cycle. The amount of money you have accumulated will determine whether you need a team of advisors. Be sure you are working with the right financial professionals for where you are in your financial life cycle.

Just as the advice you seek for your health and well-being may include a team of doctors, each providing specific expertise, you want to include a team of financial professionals for your optimal financial health and well-being. Assemble a team of experts representing the types of products you want as part of your overall retirement plan.

In the end, *you* must lead your wealth and financial well-being. Do not delegate this leadership role to any of your advisors. This does not mean you should try to become the expert on the financial products you want in your retirement plans, but it does mean that you need to have a fundamental understanding of how each product works and the trade-offs those products represent.

Sadly, many pre-retirees spend more time planning their next vacation than they do their financial future. Sometimes we don't do better because we don't know better. Knowing better is completely within your control. Invest the time in your retirement plan *now*. Better plans get better results regardless of how much you start with or when you start. Here's how you begin to choose today.

> In our working years, the purpose of money is accumulation for the future. When the future arrives, the purpose of money is spending to support the present.
> Change in purpose may require a different team with different tools to thrive in a different time.
>
> ~Judi Snyder

The first step in creating a better retirement plan is defining your money rules. These rules will help guide you in selecting the types of financial products you want in your retirement plans. Key components of money rules include purpose, participation, risk approach, productivity, and tax benefits.

Purpose

In section one we learned how to define our new purpose, something many of us never thought much about until becoming retired loomed around the corner. Thinking about the purpose of our money is even more uncommon. Not knowing the purpose of our money prevents us from measuring how successful our financial products or strategies are going to be for a successful financial future. Design a purpose-driven portfolio that allocates the appropriate amount of dollars between the various purposes based on your circumstances, concerns, and goals. The various purposes for your money could most simply be classified in one of seven categories:

1. **Liquidity**—Products that provide liquidity, such as savings accounts, money markets, and cash value life insurance.
2. **Growth**—Products that provide for the growth of your principal over a mid- to long-term horizon, such as stocks and real estate.
3. **Current Income**—Products that provide current income, such as dividend-paying stocks or life insurance, interest-bearing accounts, and annuity payments.
4. **Future Income**—Products that provide income at some future date, such as retirement accounts (401k, 403b, IRA) and annuities.
5. **Legacy**—Products that provide funds for beneficiaries at your death, such as life insurance, annuities, and trust accounts.
6. **Charity**—Products that provide current or future contributions to charities, such as charitable lead trusts and charitable remainder trusts.
7. **Protection**—Products that provide protection against the many risks you may face in retirement, such as loss of income, longevity, death, and long-term care.

Some products may cover more than one purpose. Understanding the purpose of each product in your overall retirement plan can provide the necessary insight to optimizing your plans.

Participation

Participation should be another key consideration in your financial money rules. How much of your time for active management is required? What types of experience and expertise are necessary to manage each financial product? This is a particularly important consideration for executives, business owners, and retirees. Ask yourself these questions:

1) Do you have the expertise?
2) Do you have the time?
3) Is that how you want to spend your time?

Keep in mind, even the most passive of investments require periodic review and oversight by you. Abdicating responsibility for leading your retirement plan can result in disappointment, frustration, and financial devastation.

Risk

All financial products have some type and level of risk. Even hiding cash under the mattress subjects your money to risk of loss from theft, fire, earned interest, or forgetting where you put it. Every financial product represents a tradeoff between different aspects of the investment including liquidity, principal protection, upside potential, and tax benefits. Here are the four most utilized approaches to dealing with risk in the financial products included in your retirement plans:

1. **Avoid**—You can avoid the risk of losing your principal by placing funds into a savings account. The trade-off: The return is low and may not keep ahead of the rate of inflation, decreasing your purchasing power over time.

2. **Accept**—You can accept the risk of losing your principal by placing funds into the stock market. The trade-off: The potential for higher returns comes with the possibility of losing some or all your principal.

3. **Manage**—You can manage the risk (or more often pay someone else to manage the risk) by placing your funds under management of a financial professional. The trade-off: You pay for the management regardless of

whether you gain or lose (theoretically you have a better opportunity for gains).

4. **Transfer**—You can transfer the risk to another party, either for a fee or for a portion of the upside return. The trade-off: You give up a portion of the potential upside for the ability to eliminate some or all the downside.

Another important aspect of this discussion relates to the concepts of risk tolerance and risk capacity. Both are important, but they address very different aspects of risk. Risk tolerance focuses on your emotional strength. How do you feel emotionally about risk? Can you sleep at night knowing your money is at risk? Does it bother you? Risk capacity focuses on your ability to recover financially from a loss. Do you have sufficient additional assets or future income or time to recover from a loss of principal? Are you confident you can recover from a potential loss?

Emotion always trumps logic. Just because you may have the capacity to accept risk does not mean you have the emotional strength to endure the uncertainty. Many retirees have chosen not to accept as much risk even if they have the capacity for it. For them, the peace of mind of not losing money is worth more than the potential gain by placing their money at risk. Each of us must create the balance between risk and safety that allows us to sleep at night. We call this state of mind "sleep equity." You can sleep at night because you're not worried about losing your money.

Productivity or Projected Returns

What potential rate of return are you seeking from your various financial products? If the purpose of investing is to maintain or grow your purchasing power, focus an appropriate portion of your financial products on growth, after considering your risk tolerance and risk capacity. Have a target return for each of the different financial products in your overall financial plan along with the corresponding blended return for the entire portfolio of products. Remember to balance the tradeoffs between different aspects of each financial product and aim to balance the tradeoffs to your financial temperament.

Tax Benefits

Although we never recommend making decisions on which financial products to include in your retirement savings plan based on tax benefits, we always recommend understanding the tax implications of the financial products you are considering. Every financial product comes with tax consequences. Some provide a tax deduction, some tax deferral, some tax-free withdrawals. Although there is no one-size-fits-all advice with respect to which financial products are most beneficial to your situation, understand the tax treatment of each product and balance that treatment with the other aspects of your retirement goals.

Defining your money rules will create a template you can use to review any financial product. Your template is defined in advance and away from the heat of the moment when you're deciding on a specific financial product. Your template can change over time, and it makes your decision process more efficient and effective. It provides a great shield to protect you from being sold on a product that is not right for you. If, upon review, you determine the recommended product is not congruent with your money rules, you can respond with a quick and decisive "no."

Build Your Retirement Team

We always advocate for cooperative money, not competitive money. We believe that no single advisor can be an expert on all financial products. We further believe that all advisors are biased toward the products they recommend, and they should be. You want advisors and financial professionals on your team who are experts in the products you want to include in your overall retirement portfolio. These experts not only know the features and benefits of the product, but also have the experience and insights on how to best use the products for your situation.

Always hire the expert. You don't want to serve as on-the-job training material for your advisor or financial professional. If you needed surgery or another critical medical procedure, you would most likely select a doctor with the most experience and expertise. If you needed a knee replacement, which would you prefer: the general surgeon who does one knee replacement a year, or the sports medicine orthopedic surgeon who does fifteen every week for top professional athletes? The same approach may apply to your financial advice. If you need an estate plan, hire an expert who specializes in estate plans, not a generalist who practices a little bit of everything. Most large firms have associates who focus in one area of expertise. Confirm that your advisor is truly an expert in the products you want and not just an "I can do that too" practitioner.

Beware of zealots. Anytime someone says this is the *only* solution or way to accomplish something, run the other way. There are always multiple potential solutions to any problem, and each will most likely represent certain trade-offs between the risks and benefits. Understand the trade-offs of each solution and select that which best balances them to make you comfortable. Equally, beware of advisors and financial professionals who make broad-brush assessments of their competition and their products. Every industry has great advisors, average advisors, and bad advisors and every asset class has outstanding products, average products, and terrible products. All advisors and financial professionals are paid, either by fees or commission, and there is no method more virtuous than another. If they are not providing their clients with the best service, they will fail, not because of how they are compensated but because they didn't provide value in the service they promised. In the end, the best product solution for you will depend on your circumstances, risk tolerance, and personal preferences. Choose the best tool for the problem you want to solve.

The deal of the century comes around every month. Don't be pressured into moving faster than you are comfortable with because the offer is only good for two more days. Don't be caught up in "you have to do this by a deadline" or else. Complete your due diligence, move at your own pace, and only move forward when *you* are 100 percent comfortable.

Don't fix things that aren't broken. Certainly, there are portions of your current plans that are in good order and should not be "fixed" by a new advisor or financial professional. Become concerned when an advisor or financial professional recommends changes to your entire retirement plan, especially when the recommendation involves moving everything to the advisor's or financial professional's proprietary products.

Don't change for "about the same." If things aren't broken, then leave them alone. Only consider changing when making the changes will clearly put you in a compellingly better situation. Change is the single most difficult thing for human beings to do and changes involving money are doubly so. Make sure you clearly understand the compelling reasons for making any changes to your retirement savings products.

Every product represents trade-offs. Often the trade-offs revolve around concepts like liquidity, principal protection, guarantees, focus on income, growth or both, tax implications, and time horizon. There is no perfect product for everyone and there is no perfect product for all your money. Trade-offs are neither good nor bad in general, but they could be good or bad for you, depending on your circumstances, concerns, and goals. Take time to understand how each product fits into your overall retirement plans. Frequently asked questions can be misleading because they may be designed to lead you down the road to the provider of the products to arrive at a manipulated conclusion. To get their expert recommendations, ask your financial professionals what you ought to know that no one is asking about. We refer to these as the "should ask" or "must ask" questions. You want to know what questions the experts would ask for each product you're interested in and how it affects your overall retirement plan.

Seek referrals, ask for references, and trust your gut. Referrals can be an excellent approach to building your retirement team if you understand the true definition of a referral. A referral is an introduction to an expert by someone you know and trust who has had direct experience with the advisor or financial professional being referred to you, and they can validate the professional's expertise and ability to solve your problem. You should interview the advisor first to determine whether they hold similar values and whether there exists the necessary chemistry to form a successful advisor–client relationship. Don't be afraid to ask questions, and don't work with any advisor or financial professional who talks over your head or is condescending toward you. Trust your gut feeling. And verify by seeking references who can validate this new financial professional from both an experience and results perspective.

Get a Second Opinion (or Two or Three)

In healthcare, it is quite common to seek a second opinion before beginning or continuing a treatment plan. Although the goal of all doctors is the same—the well-being of the patient—the approaches, plans, and tools to achieve that outcome may be different. In a 2017 Mayo Clinic study, *The Journal of Evaluation in Clinical Practice*, James Naessens, Sc.D. found the following:

> *"Many patients seek a second opinion or diagnosis confirmation before treatment for a complex condition. In a new study, researchers report that as many as 88 percent of those patients go home with a new or refined diagnosis — changing their care plan and potentially their lives. Conversely, only 12 percent receive confirmation that the original diagnosis was complete and correct."*

What does this have to do with your retirement plans? Everything! Isn't your "wealth care" just as important as your health care? If the optimal plan for your well-being changed 88 percent of the time in preserving your vitality, why would you not want the same improvements for your prosperity? The retirement landscape continues to change quickly, requiring retirees and near retirees to keep up with the new information, options, and opportunities. The bottom line is to get a second opinion or, at a minimum, have a second conversation with your current team of financial professionals and discuss your changing circumstances. Don't assume that your advisory team is aware of your changes in circumstances or goals. Persistent proactive communication is critical for your advisory team to fulfill their role in recommending the most appropriate strategies for your financial success.

Financial Life Cycle

We all evolve through our physical and emotional life cycles. Physically, our bodies develop, grow stronger, hit a peak, and then slowly decline until our passing. Emotionally, we progress through a similar cycle. We mature through our teenage years into adulthood and eventually translate our experiences into wisdom and contentment. We also have a financial life cycle. The focus of our financial goals, the types of financial products to which we allocate our retirement savings, and the remaining time horizon also evolve. The purpose of our retirement savings and our capacity to handle risk also change over that life cycle. When we are younger, our focus is primarily on growth because we are willing to accept the risk in exchange for the higher potential gains. There are two main reasons we can accept the risk early in our financial life cycle: time horizon and earned income. We have time to recover from losses in the market and we can replace losses from our paychecks.

As we progress through our financial life cycle, our time horizon shortens until we need to utilize some portion of our retirement accounts for income. Our ability to replace losses from our paycheck declines and is virtually eliminated upon retirement. Even if we choose to "make dough with what we know" and continue working, chances are we won't work the hours or make the income that we did in the height of our career. This scenario led to a formula to determine the balance between at-risk financial products and safe financial products called the "Rule of 100." There are modern variations to this philosophy such as using the age 110 or 120, but the subtraction formula is the same.

🐚 Simply stated, subtract your age from one hundred, one hundred ten or one hundred twenty.

🐚 The remaining number represents the approximate amount of your overall retirement savings that should be at risk in the market.

For example, using the "rule of 100", a forty-year-old person may consider 60 percent at-risk financial products and 40 percent safe. A sixty-year-old person would consider 40 percent at-risk financial products and 60 percent safe.

🐚 Some planners use the age you want to retire for this calculation rather than age one hundred. If you plan to retire at seventy, you will subtract your current age from seventy to determine the percentage amount of your overall retirement savings that should be allocated to at-risk financial products.

The more time you have, the more risk you can manage; you can focus more of your retirement resources on growth. The less time you have, the less risk you can accept; the focus shifts to preservation and income generation.

The purpose of your retirement savings shifts from growth to income. The time horizon shrinks from long to short. The amount of liquidity moves from small to larger. Because a significant loss of retirement savings close to your planned retirement date may delay or degrade your retirement plans, your risk capacity declines over time.

Remember these two truths:

1. The purpose of investing is to maintain and grow your purchasing power for years to come. Your first objective is to keep up with inflation. Next, you want to increase your purchasing power to yield the retirement plan you want.

2. Money will make you more of what you are. Money will not make you happy, but it will give you more choices, and more choices are always a good thing.

Is there a mismatch or disconnect between your current retirement savings allocation and where you are in your financial life cycle? Has the purpose for your retirement savings changed? Has it shifted from growth to preservation and income generation? Has your time horizon from when you would need to draw on your retirement saving shortened? Are you now closer to retiring then further away? Has the amount of risk you can accept or want to accept decreased? These are important questions that you ought to ask yourself periodically. Sometimes we get caught up in the routine of daily life and don't address our changing needs.

Choosersizes – Control Your Financial House or Others Will

🐚 Complete your money rules.
🐚 Identify and build your retirement team and assess where you need to add experts.
🐚 Get a second opinion.

*Download the companion workbook
www.BecomingRetiredishWorkbook.com

Chapter 8

WHAT IS YOUR MOST IMPORTANT ROI?

When you read the acronym ROI, what comes to mind? Most will answer, return on investment. Although that is an important ROI, it's not the *most important*. As you approach becoming retiredish, your most important ROI is reliability of income.

Think about it. If you had a reliable source of income for the remainder of your life and that of your spouse or partner, how would you feel? Virtually everyone says the same thing: secure. As you look to transition from work to retirement—trading time for money—the type of income ought to shift from active to passive. The retirement products you have chosen and funded—along with other sources of income like pensions, Social Security, and passive business or investment income—should now provide the retirement paycheck that enables you to experience the retirement lifestyle you desire. The reliability of this retirement paycheck will directly impact your happiness and longevity.

A 2020 article by Tom Hegna, economist, author, and retirement expert, outlines the importance of reliability of income for retirees and arrives at the following conclusion: People with a guaranteed lifetime income source tend to be happier and live longer. According to Hegna, his conclusion is not an opinion; it's a mathematical, scientific, and economic fact. Visit www.tomhegna.com for more unbiased financial education specific to retirement. The data and insights provided from his research span as far back as the Roman Empire all the way through today's PhDs.

Guaranteed Pay Checks and Play Checks Lead to Happiness in Retirement

Let's start with a question: Who are the happiest retirees you know? I'll bet it's those who are retired from the military, government, teaching, and firefighting. It's those who have pensions. A *Wall Street Journal* headline reinforces this perception: "The Secret to a Happier Retirement is Friends, Neighbors and a Fixed Annuity." The article went on to say that the happiest people in retirement were those who were surrounded by friends and had sources of guaranteed lifetime income. Happiness in retirement is based almost 100 percent on guaranteed lifetime income, not assets.

It's not just American retirees who feel this way. *Time* magazine found the same thing in Great Britain. Their headline read, "Lifetime Income Stream Key to Retirement Happiness: a new study in a land of grumps reveals that retirees with a guaranteed lifetime income stream can find true happiness." They went on to say that securing at least a base level of lifetime income should be every retiree's priority—at least if they want to live happily ever after.

The American College recently wrote an article titled "How Annuities Can Increase Happiness in Retirement." It was found that, "A stable income is often the difference between living well and living in a state of perpetual worry. And this truth doesn't change just because someone retires." In addition, "When clients know how much income they will receive every month for life, they know what kind of housing and activities they can afford, allowing them to choose the lifestyle that makes them happiest."

Michael Finke and Wade Pfau are two Ph.D.'s who have studied retirement. They recently wrote a white paper, "It's More than Money," in which they found that happiness is tied directly to confidence: "Certainty provides confidence. This is one of the reasons that retirees who've incorporated income annuities into their retirement planning report higher levels of satisfaction."

Longevity in Retirement

The Roman Empire issued "annuas" to ensure people wouldn't run out of money, meaning that this concept of guaranteed lifetime income is as old as dirt. Although those original Roman recipients are no longer collecting, the concept has stood the test of time. How does it impact *your* longevity? Let's take a look.

Jane Austen included this commentary on lifetime guaranteed income in her 1811 classic, *Sense and Sensibility*: "If you observe, people always live forever when there is an annuity to be paid to them... The annuity is a serious business; it comes over and over every year, and there is no getting rid of it."

In the Journal of Financial Services Professionals, 2018, Patrick C. Tricker wrote an article entitled "Annuities and Moral Hazard, Can Longevity Insurance Increase Longevity?" According to Tricker, in the United States, a sixty-five-year-old male who purchases a life annuity can expect to live about 20 percent longer than a sixty-five-year-old male who does not. (*Journal of Financial Service Professionals*, July 2018). Tricker claims that people who have guaranteed lifetime income tend to have less stress. They also worry less. They watch what they eat, they exercise a little more, and they see the doctor when they aren't feeling well so they pre-empt illness from progressing to fatal stages. All these little things tend to cause them to live longer.

In a surprising study published by the University of Chicago in the Journal of Political Economy, *Old Age Longevity and Mortality Contingent Claims,* Tomas j. Philipson and Gary S. Becker found that those who purchased a lifetime income annuity tended to live longer—and not just because they are the kind of people who have the money to buy annuities to start with. Annuities that provide an income you can never outlive, pay until death, even if you exhausted all of your original principal and interest is apparently that little extra incentive of the annuity payout that keeps people going.

Can we now agree that focusing on your most important ROI—reliability of income—yields the best results for both happiness and longevity in retirement? And a better question, why has this become such a big issue for Baby Boomer retirees?

WHAT IS YOUR MOST IMPORTANT ROI?

The Duping of America's Employees

Prior to 1990, pensions were the most common type of retirement plan offered to employees. Known by IRS nomenclature as a defined benefit plan, the pension was a company-sponsored benefit. It was wholly funded by the company, which paid all fees, managed risk, and converted funds into a guaranteed lifetime income for employees and their spouses. The guaranteed payout amount of a lifetime pension was determined by years of employment, earnings, and age at retirement.

About 1990, employers began to shift the type of retirement plan offered to their employees from a defined benefit plan (a pension) to a defined contribution plan (a 401(k), 403(b), 457(b), or another employer sponsored plan). With a defined contribution plan, the contribution made by the employee is defined but not the outcome at retirement age. The employer may provide some level of matching funds, but is no longer responsible for fully funding the plan, paying the fees, managing the risk, or converting the balance of funds into a lifetime pension payment for the employee and spouse. The employee is now responsible for all these activities. How much training did you receive on risk management, stock market investing, and income distribution planning?

If you're like most Americans, your answer is probably none. You can easily see why this was a good deal for your company, for Wall Street, and for the IRS. For you? Not so much. Your employer just passed the liability and expense for the pension to you. At most, it costs them a small amount to set up the employer-sponsored plans and the amount of a small match. Clearly a win for corporate America. Wall Street benefited by the increase in the number of investors in their products. Prior to 1990, fewer than one out of every three households in American had a direct investment in the stock market. By 2020, almost two out of three households were invested in the stock market. Even those under the age of 35 saw a significant shift in stock market participation, from less than 22 percent to more than 41 percent. Most of these new investors were captive to their plans, meaning they had a limited choice as to which type of products, providers, and companies they could allocate their retirement savings. Clearly a win for Wall Street. And the IRS? Now they could tax your withdrawals at ordinary income rates, penalize you for early withdrawals, and tax your beneficiaries on any remaining retirement savings. Uncle Sam always gets paid, and usually first!

If happiness and longevity in retirement are directly linked to the amount of guaranteed lifetime income you have and one of the primary sources of guaranteed income has been eliminated, doesn't that sound like a recipe for failure and uncertainty? The good news is that better plans get better results, no matter when you start or how much you start with. How can you design a better plan? Let's start at the beginning with understanding your cash flow.

Know Thy Numbers... Cash Flow is Royalty

Years ago, when my husband, Jeff, and I were bantering on our radio show, we would often have what we called "Mars–Venus" moments. You may remember the book by John Gray, *Men are from Mars and Women are from Venus*. The key point of the book is the importance of being able to speak your partner's language. For example, on one show, Jeff said that we had been together for four major league baseball seasons. I replied, no, we had been together for eight Nordstrom's semi-annual sales. We had another Mars–Venus moment when it came to our description of the importance of cash flow. Jeff would say that cash flow is king. I would proclaim that cash flow is queen. He would respond with king! No, queen! I guess it depends on who you believe ranks higher, the king or the queen, but we finally agreed that cash flow is royalty.

Cash flow is simply your income minus your expenses. Your income can be categorized as either guaranteed or hopeful. Your expenses can be classified as either required or desired. The difference represents your discretionary income or, more simply stated, income you can decide where and when to spend or allocate. The name of the game is to create as much discretionary income as possible. To optimize this equation, you will need to know your numbers. What are your sources of guaranteed and hopeful income and how will they change over time? What are your required and desired expenses and how will they change over time? And do you have a positive or negative certainty gap?

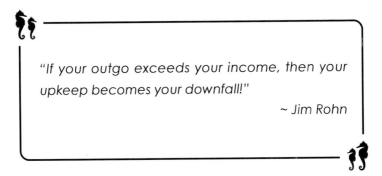

"If your outgo exceeds your income, then your upkeep becomes your downfall!"

~ Jim Rohn

Guaranteed Income and Hopeful Income

Guaranteed income includes pension payments, Social Security payments, guaranteed interest payments on bonds, CDs or savings accounts, dividend payments from stocks or mutual funds, certain rent or lease payments, annuity payments, and any other contractually guaranteed recurring payment. Keep in mind that all these guaranteed sources have the possibility of failing, but based on history the probability of failure is low. Hopeful income includes stock or mutual fund payments from portfolio gains, oil and gas royalties, interest on secured or unsecured promissory notes, and gains from speculative investments. The more guaranteed sources of income you can create, the happier and longer your retirement will be. It's not recommended that your retirement should count on the hopeful income plan, so let's look at how we can provide the certainty of guaranteed sources of income.

Required and Desired Expenses

Required expenses are non-discretionary expenses. Non-discretionary expenses include mortgage payments, property taxes, utilities, food, etc. They're non-discretionary in that if you choose not to pay them, then the service will no longer be provided. If you don't pay your electric bill, they turn the electricity off. It's not discretionary. Likewise, you can't choose to stop eating and still live. Food is non-discretionary. You need food to be able to maintain life, although quality and selection may be a function of your income. Desired expenses represent the amount of money you would like to have, including your non-discretionary expenses. Discretionary expenses include travel, hobbies, presents, and charity. These types of expenditure add to the joy in your life, but they aren't required to survive.

Both types of expenses should be reviewed and updated periodically for necessity and optimization. Necessity means that the expense is truly necessary. Necessity can change over time as your circumstances and technology evolve. For example, years ago we all had a home phone. We paid an extra expense to have a home phone. Today, it's not a necessity. Most people have cell phones and have gotten rid of their home phones along with the corresponding expense. Cable TV would be another example. Optimization focuses on efficiency and making sure all your expenses are adjusted regularly to benefit from new programs and offerings. In other words, have you shopped the market for that expense and found that you truly have the best value for your dollar? For example, you may have noticed that certain service or product prices start high and come down over time as competition heats up, yet those companies don't bother to inform you their prices have dropped. Cell phone service, streaming services, and homeowner and automobile insurance are all examples of this phenomenon.

The Certainty Gap and its Impact on Your Retirement

The following stacked bar chart captures the relationship between your guaranteed and hopeful income and your required and desired expenses. Please note that by stacking your hopeful income on top of your guaranteed income, you can visually see your total potential income. Likewise, by stacking your desired expenses on top of your required expenses, you can visually see your total potential expenses. And by viewing both stacked bar charts on the same page, you can see your certainty gap.

Figure 1 demonstrates a negative certainty gap. Your required expenses exceed your guaranteed income. You are now placed in a situation where you must rely on your hopeful income just to cover your necessary expenses. This can potentially impact your liquid reserves negatively, causing them to be depleted more quickly as you make withdrawals to cover your required expenses. Over time, the lower (or non-existent) liquid reserve may also lead to greater stress and less happiness in retirement.

Figure 2 demonstrates a positive certainty gap. Your guaranteed income exceeds your required expenses. You are now in a scenario where you can cover some of your desired expenses from guaranteed income without the need to tap into your hopeful income or your liquid reserves. You can even choose to augment your liquid reserves by depositing some of your hopeful income into your reserves. This positive certainty gap can also lead to greater happiness and less stress in retirement.

CERTAINTY GAP

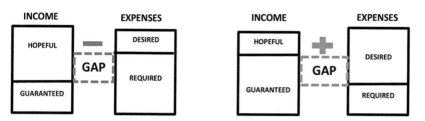

The No-Pension Dilemma

We all got duped. Corporations, Wall Street, and our government collaborated in shifting the primary retirement source of income from company-sponsored pensions to employee-funded 401(k), 403(b), and IRA plans. This shift has created a pension dilemma for *all* Americans. What to do when faced with a dilemma? Make "dilemmonade." That's right, you can turn your dilemma into dilemmonade, but first you must understand which pension dilemmas you are facing.

For most retirees, their pension dilemma is that they don't have a pension. Their employers shifted to offering a 401k or other similar company-sponsored retirement plan. Retirees who worked for companies that did not offer a retirement plan or who were self-employed face the same dilemma. According to Bankrate, less than 13 percent of Americans have pensions. Although this impacts approximately 87 percent of us, there is some good news. Did you know that you can buy or create your own pension, often with more benefits and flexibility than the old company-sponsored plans?

The best financial product solution for this dilemma is an annuity. In fact, most of the traditional pension plans were funded with annuities, which are products of insurance companies. I know, I know. You have been told by advisors, family members, friends, and other so-called experts that annuities are lousy investments. You will be surprised to learn that I agree with that statement.

First, insurance products such as annuities are not investments. They are insurance products. Insurance products allow you to transfer your risk to a company that specializes in mitigating those risks. This contractual guarantee is dependent on the financial strength and claims-paying ability of the insurance company. History has demonstrated that insurance companies are extremely conservative, operate on actuarial science and the law of large numbers, are regulated by each State's department of insurance, and are reviewed and rated by outside agencies. Although no company can guarantee their survival and thriving into perpetuity, insurance companies have a track record that indicates they will most likely be the last ones standing.

Secondly, saying that annuities are a lousy investment would be like saying a screwdriver is a lousy hammer. It depends on what problem you are trying to solve. Can we agree that for any problem you are trying to solve, you should employ the best tool to solve it? If you are like most retirees, creating a retirement paycheck and running out of money in retirement are two of your biggest challenges. The only financial product that can guarantee both your future payment and that you don't outlive your money is an annuity. You can transfer your longevity risk to an insurance company by purchasing an annuity contract. But wait, there's more.

Today's annuity contracts can provide important guarantees and benefits beyond longevity protections. These additional benefits can include guaranteed increasing future income and guarantees that every dollar contributed, along with all the gains received, will be paid to you or your beneficiary. They also offer special provisions for your spouse including joint life income, and the ability to take over the contract as their own, and even potential additional benefits when faced with a long-term care situation. Most importantly, they offer the opportunity to change your mind. Unlike the old traditional pension plans where your decisions were irrevocable, today's annuity contracts offer the ability to start and stop your income payments and an opportunity to walk away with a lump sum.

The Have-Pension Dilemma

For those fortunate enough to have a pension, there are still several dilemmas that must be addressed. The most important of these would include the decisions to take the monthly payments or a lump sum (if available), to take monthly payments on a single-life, joint-life, or life-plus-period-certain basis, when to start receiving the monthly payments, and whether to take inflation protection.

Many companies are now offering pension holders the option of a guaranteed series of monthly payments or a lump sum benefit that can be taken in cash (taxable now) or rolled over to an IRA (tax deferred). Determining which would be in your best interest will depend on two key factors: your desire or need for additional guaranteed sources of income and the availability of financial products that could provide a pension with more benefits and flexibility than traditional pensions. Utilize the expertise of a financial professional to help you choose wisely. This decision will have an important impact on both your happiness and longevity in retirement.

Most companies will offer pension holders options for guaranteed income that will be paid to the pensioner or to their spouse and beneficiaries. One of the most difficult decisions for a pension holder can involve spousal continuation. The loss of a spouse is emotionally devastating and can be financially damaging as well. Although the surviving spouse will keep the larger of the couple's Social Security payments, the smaller will be discontinued. Other sources of income may also be eliminated upon the death of a spouse. Typically, household expenses are not reduced significantly after one spouse dies—certainly not by half. This places pressure on the decision between single- or joint-life payout for a pension (joint-life pays out at a reduced rate when compared to single life). If there is a significant difference in age between spouses, the dilemma may be further magnified.

One potential solution to this dilemma is to choose the higher single-life payout option and purchase a life insurance policy on the pension holder. The death benefit payout could be used to replace the income lost at the time of the pension holder's death. The benefit of this approach is that often the net pension payment (higher single-life payout minus the premium expense for the life insurance policy) is larger than the joint-life payout option. It also protects the pension holder from taking the smaller joint-life payout only to outlive a spouse and be locked into the lower payout for the balance of their life. If the spouse does pre-decease the pension holder, the pension holder can continue with the higher monthly pension and decide whether to continue the life insurance policy for their children or surrender the policy for any cash value and increase their net monthly payment to the full single-life payout amount.

Another option to protect a pension holder's beneficiaries (spouse, children, or others) is to take a lower payout amount in exchange for a guaranteed number of years over which the pension payments will be made. This option is known as "life plus X years certain" where X equals the number of guaranteed years to be paid to the original pensioner or designated beneficiaries. For example, if you were to elect the life plus 20 years certain option, the pension will be paid for as long as you live with a minimum payout of twenty years. If you were to pass away after the tenth year, the balance of ten years would be paid to your beneficiaries. The greater the number of years, the X, the smaller the monthly payments. You can also calculate the break-even point if your company offers you a lump sum option.

Analyzing family health history to project your life expectancy and that of your spouse, in concert with your personal temperament and crunching the numbers, will provide insight into which option to select.

Many companies offer pension holders the option of when to start their pension payments. This decision is impacted by your target retirement start date, the growth (if any) in the pension payment amount if delayed to a later date, and the potential impact on your taxes. A few companies continue to offer pension holders the option of level income starting at a larger monthly payment or increasing income starting at a smaller monthly payment. Selecting which option is best for you will be influenced by the level of guaranteed income you will have from all sources and by how your ongoing plan will deal with inflation. Inflation is a critical issue that every retiree must have a plan to address.

The "I Don't Know" Pension Dilemma

A common scenario I consistently see with clients is not knowing about pension benefits. Before I became involved in financial services, I was an executive in corporate America. I worked for large Fortune 50 companies and had the blessing of receiving pensions from those companies. But even I was surprised to learn that I had a pension I was unaware of. I mistakenly assumed that because I hadn't been with the company for five years, I didn't have a pension. I rolled over my 401(k) and thought that was all I had to do. It wasn't until years later, when that company was purchased by another company, that I discovered I had a pension benefit. I make it a point to encourage everyone to make some phone calls and check in with human resources on potential benefits.

For example, a client who was recently downsized came to me to roll over her 403(b). I asked whether she had pension benefits and she said no. I was leery of her no because it was a government position, and I was positive they had a pension benefit. We called them together and discovered that she did indeed have a pension, it would pay over $2,000 monthly, she could begin as early as sixty-two, and waiting longer wouldn't increase the payout. Cha-ching!

Here's another example. A client lost her husband when he was fifty-eight years old. When she turned sixty, she elected to take his Social Security benefit so she could allow her Social Security benefit to grow until she turns seventy. When the first payment of her deceased husband's Social Security benefit initiated, it triggered notification to all his previous employers. This was a second marriage for both, and she did not know all the companies he had worked for early in his career. Within a month, she received notification from a previous employer that her deceased spouse had a pension. He had listed his first wife as the beneficiary, but his first wife was deceased. My client provided the company with her marriage certificate and her husband's death certificate and was offered her choice of a lump sum pension benefit or multiple payments. I'm sure her deceased husband had no idea of this pension benefit, or he would have updated the beneficiary when they married.

Whether you are in the no-pension, have-pension, or I-don't-know pension dilemma, there are solutions. Your advisors and financial professionals can help you make the perfect choices. However, *you* must begin by knowing your numbers so they can guide you with their expertise. It is also *your* responsibility to keep your financial team up to date on changes in your circumstances. I think we can agree, the known feels better than the unknown.

Adopting a Spend-Shift Mindset Doesn't Mean You Are a Spendthrift

Bravo, you've done a fantastic job of saving your money over your working years. You've likely accumulated your savings by adopting a mantra that goes something like this: this is money I can't touch, this is earmarked for my future, or some variation of these words. Remember back in chapter two when we discussed beliefs and how they become part of our automatic subconscious behaviors? Well, here is the flip side of your saving mindset—you now have difficulty spending your money. You wonder whether the future is now, or should you wait a little bit longer? You worry about becoming a spendthrift if you spend your money on things you deem unnecessary and risk not having enough money for the important things the rest of your days. It becomes a bit cloudy as to what is necessary and important and what is frivolous. We haven't exercised our spending muscles for 40 years, so every decision feels extravagant, as though you are becoming a spendthrift.

A spendthrift is a person who spends money in an extravagant, irresponsible way. Having a purpose and a well-thought-out plan is *not* being a spendthrift. However, developing a spending mindset does require a shift in thinking to accompany the shift in your retiredish years.

Warren Buffet said, *"Someone is sitting in the shade today because someone planted a tree a long time ago."* You are now in the shade stage; it's time to stop planting trees and enjoy the fruits of your labor, the shade.

Uncertainty is the root cause of retiredish anxiety. Uncertain life span, uncertain medical expenses, uncertain market conditions, uncertain taxation, uncertain inflation, and uncertainty about our ability, or desire, to work as we age are all factors that cause many retiredish people to spend their retirement assets more slowly. Sudipto Banerjee, Employee Benefit Research Institute, Washington, DC who authored *Change in Household Spending After Retirement: Results from a Longitudinal Sample,* Nov 19, 2015, found that in the first two decades of retirement, most retirees don't spend down their assets. "This behavior is not limited to those with lower levels [of] assets, to the contrary, of all the subgroups studied, pensioners have the lowest asset spend-down rates."

As a Certified Financial Transitionist, I have worked with many clients on transitions that include all types of money events, including anticipated retirement, inheritance, loss of spouse or partner, settlements, and even windfalls such as lottery winnings. My observations prompted me to conduct a small base study with our clients who had difficulty spending when they reached their golden age of retirement, and some common findings were as follows:

WHAT IS YOUR MOST IMPORTANT ROI?

🐚 Uncertainty about outliving money due to unforeseen world conditions.

🐚 Fear of missing out, otherwise known as FOMO, on high returns during a booming market.

🐚 Paralysis when transition to spending was required.

There are products and strategies to help you create more certainty around world conditions, FOMO, and paralysis. Recognize that you now have a new job: Create a purpose-driven portfolio that will provide you with the peace of mind you desire.

Understanding the components of certainty is key and will help you build a framework. Adopt strategies to guarantee cash flow, determine reserves, and provide insurance so you can successfully transition to the shift in purpose during the homestretch of retirement from:

🐚 Growth → Preservation

🐚 Accumulation → Distribution

🐚 Risk → Safety

🐚 Uncertainty → Certainty

A successful financial transition would include continuously pushing your retirement savings to *greater protection, greater productivity,* and *greater purpose.* Following this principle will help mitigate the five biggest risks to your retirement dreams:

1. Pension Dilemma — providing a known guaranteed retirement paycheck that you can never outlive.

2. Inflation — providing increasing income to keep ahead of inflation.

3. Taxes — providing options to eliminate the risk of future increases in taxes.

4. Market Volatility — providing options to eliminate losses due to market declines while still being able to take advantage of the market rebounds.
5. Long Term Care — providing options to help offset the potential devastating impact of a long-term care situation.

Healthy Compartmentalization

In psychology, compartmentalization is defined as a defense mechanism whereby someone suppresses their thoughts and emotions. It is not always done consciously, but this can often justify or defend a person's level of engagement in certain behaviors. In other words, we put it in the drawer and deal with it later. Compartmentalization is a defense mechanism used to avoid cognitive dissonance, which is the anxiety resulting from having conflicting beliefs. Healthy compartmentalization helps us to perform under pressure and maintain some semblance of normalcy during difficult situations. The challenge arises when compartmentalization becomes disconnection. Disconnecting from the very thing you put in the drawer for later can lead to paralysis, and paralysis prevents you from making mindful timely decisions that serve your best interest.

Many people I've coached over the years have shared that they put their financial statements in an "I'll get to it soon" pile and never really get to it until tax time. This is a perfect example of how compartmentalization becomes disconnection. Waiting until the last possible minute to address any issue most likely leaves great solutions in the dust. Making decisions in the heat of the moment is never optimal.

How Do You Exercise Your Spending Muscles?

If you exercised your physical muscles for forty-plus years you would be pretty darn buff and you would have some amazing muscle memory going on. As most personal fitness trainers will tell you, to keep your muscles optimized, you need to confuse them regularly so they don't become used to the same exercises. Confusing your body's muscles boosts performance, and this confusion is achieved through a strategic workout plan designed to optimally condition your muscles that enhance your physical fitness. Transitioning to a spending mindset is similar. Your saving mindset of "this is money I can't touch" causes confusion once you enter the spending stage. It will force to you revisit your money paradigm if you want to keep moving forward. Mindset confusion can act as a nudge that encourages you to consider change. When you are confused you seek information, and that new knowledge will bring clarity. Clarity will enable you to transform your new knowledge into action. First you introduce mindset confusion by asking your mind to do something counterintuitive to being a good steward with your money. When you properly exercise your mind and gain clarity, with planning and purpose, your mindset will become stronger and healthier. Exercising both your physical and mindset muscles with strategy and purpose will lead to optimal physical and financial fitness well into your retiredish years.

Happiness in retirement requires a mindset shift:
Saver to Spender
Developing a well-thought-out plan for the purpose
of your money will help alleviate fear of uncertainty
and allow you to make this transition.

~Judi Snyder

Take a "Wealth Care Sabbatical" — To Spend or Not to Spend

Schedule time on your calendar to research and strategize your spending. Revisit the "why." Why did you save in the first place? Engage with a thought leader, a professional, or your partner so you have some out-of-your-head viewpoints. Next, ask the following questions:

1. Are my paychecks (required) and playchecks (desired) income needs guaranteed? What is my happiness worth? Can I put a price tag on joy?
2. Do I want my beneficiaries to enjoy my money more than I do? Sure, you may want to leave your loved ones some money, but is that why you diligently saved all your working years?
3. What may happen if I spend this money now? Will it improve my life or circumstances?
4. What may happen if I don't spend this money now? What are the costs of giving up the "thing" I am considering spending money on and how will not having this affect my life?

One of these answers will feel more important to you than the other. No one can make these decisions for you. Follow your gut. Take baby steps in your spending. Do your research so you can feel good about exercising all your options.

Build your Mindful Money Map, a tool to help you balance lifestyle, wealth preservation, and wealth building. The Mindful Money Map utilizes your current resources—income (guaranteed and hopeful), expenses (required and desired), reserves, and insurance—and allocates according to your needs. By knowing cash requirements, reserves, and insurance specific to your needs, you can allocate cash flow with forethought and flow your money on autopilot. You'll want to consider financial products that are purpose driven and address liquidity, growth, income, and protection.

If you have required and desired income needs covered and still have difficulty spending money on things that bring you joy because you believe it is frivolous, try taking baby steps by doing one small thing a month that brings you joy. Harvest profit from a retirement account or earmark a specific amount of your savings to a "fun" account. You can use this for vacations, spa days, and dinners with friends. Revisit your "curious list" and start checking off the boxes. If you are credit card averse, you may want to fund a pre-paid Visa credit card and make it a point to spend down the balance on this card every year.

Life is a series of decisions. You've made good decisions to build up your nest-egg and have now entered a new phase in your financial life cycle. When you arrive at the crossroads of accumulation and distribution, you now need to make similar good decisions that allow you to enjoy the fruits of your good stewardship in retirement. This requires a mindset shift followed by new approaches and tools. It may also require you to recognize that the paralysis of letting old beliefs drive your behavior may be putting your peace of mind on hold. Take a road you haven't yet traveled and enjoy the scenic route of certainty.

Choosersizes – More Money Can't Fix Bad Spending Habits

🐚 Complete your budget worksheet to understand your required and desired income needs. Adopt a healthy transition from saving to spending by developing a plan and purpose for your savings. Evaluate home services and insurance premiums to confirm you are paying the lowest price for your required need.

🐚 Contact previous companies in which you have been employed; confirm you are up to date on your benefits and that they have your current address and beneficiaries on file.

🐚 Complete your Mindful Money Map to set your money on autopilot.

*Download the companion workbook
www.BecomingRetiredishWorkbook.com

Chapter 9

UNCLE SAM'S PLAN IS NOT YOUR JAM

It is worth mentioning again that better plans get better results, no matter when you begin or how much you start with. A great retirement doesn't happen by coincidence or chance, it happens by plan. And having a backup plan gives you more choices to realize your retirement dreams. If you only have plan A and that doesn't work out, you are now stuck. If only you had planned better and included a plan B—maybe even a plan C. By having three plans for creating your successful retirement, you have more choices. More choices provide more opportunities to succeed, which in turn yields more certainty. Planning for your retirement can expose a lot of uncertainty. Anything you can do to create more certainty will lead to a happier and most likely longer retirement.

Retirees often tell us they don't have a plan. This guarantees you will end up with the default plan and you may not like it. As the late Jim Rohn often said, *"If you don't design your own life plan, chances are you will fall into someone else's plan. And guess what they have planned for you? Not much!"* The default plan often involves relying on your family or on the government. Neither would be the preferred choice for most retirees. Who is in the best position to decide what you want in your retirement and how to respond to any challenges you will inevitably face? Your family? The government? You and your spouse or partner? Is it better to create your plans now or after you need the solution? We have always recommended pre-planning for contingencies outside the heat of the moment. Once the contingency plans are completed, they become like a plug-and-play video—take it off the bookshelf and execute the plan.

In the previous two chapters, we reviewed the importance of understanding where you are in your financial life cycle and how the advisors, strategies, financial products, and tools will change as your progress from early adulthood toward retirement and beyond. We also discussed how to create your money rules, how to build your retirement planning team, and how to recognize the value in seeking out second opinions. You learned that "cash flow is royalty" and must be your first planning priority. We asserted that your most important ROI is reliability of income, discussed how the certainty of your income can increase both your happiness and longevity in retirement, and gave suggestions for creating guaranteed sources of income. We introduced the concept of your certainty gap and explored the financial and emotional benefits of creating a positive gap. But there are several other areas of planning that will require your thoughtful consideration. There are several retirement predators looking to take a bite out of your retirement plans. Fortunately, the right plans will mitigate or eliminate these risks.

Cash Poor Purgatory

The **first key area** is liquidity. Getting a handle on your cash flow today, at retirement, and throughout retirement will determine your liquid reserve. A liquid reserve is critically important to your overall financial plan as well as your happiness in retirement. You will need funds liquid for four primary purposes. First, to provide a buffer that will smooth out the ups and downs between income and expenses from month to month. **Second,** to provide funds for emergencies that will most likely occur at some points during your retirement. The emergency could be replacing a car or air conditioner or an unexpected trip to visit family. **Third,** to provide funds to take advantage of opportunities. Investors call it "keeping your powder dry." Whether an investment or a great vacation deal, you never know when a good opportunity may present itself. Whatever the opportunity, you want to be in a position to take advantage of it. **The fourth** purpose of liquidity would be a combination of numbers two and three: the ability to help a family member or friend in their time of need. My husband and I have personally been on all sides of this dilemma. We have been there to help financially and felt blessed to do so. We have also experienced times when we couldn't help and felt powerless to make a difference in someone's life for whom we cared so deeply. Recognize your need for liquid reserves and plan accordingly by getting your amount and sources to be "just right."

The first aspect of planning your liquid reserve involves determining how much to keep liquid. Every financial product choice represents a trade-off, and funding your liquid reserve is no different. The trade-off is between liquidity and potential return. In most cases, but not all, you trade potential upside growth for liquidity. Since you need some level of liquidity, the trade-off is justified. So how much is the right amount of funds to keep liquid? The answer is, it depends. The amount of liquid funds that is right for everyone will vary, but most likely will be a function of five elements:

1. Frequency of income
2. Reliability of income
3. Number of months' worth of expenses to be covered
4. Lead-time to liquidity
5. Personal temperament

The frequency and reliability of income will impact your liquidity needs. The more frequent and reliable your income, the less liquidity is necessary. The less frequent and reliable your income, the more liquidity you will need. This will link directly back to your certainty gap. A positive certainty gap requires a lower liquid reserve while a negative certainty gap could require a larger liquid reserve.

Let's review the updated certainty gap chart below. The number of months of projected future expenses to be covered is up to each individual. Those with more frequent and reliable sources of income may choose to keep three to six months in their liquid reserve. Those with less frequent and reliable sources of income may choose to have six to twelve months in their liquid reserve. The lead-time to liquidity represents how long it takes to have access to cash following your request for the funds. A savings account is instantly liquid while a money market, mutual fund, or annuity account may require a two- to three-day time period to settle and make the funds available. Other types of accounts, like certificates of deposit, may have limited liquidity windows without an early withdrawal penalty.

CERTAINTY GAP

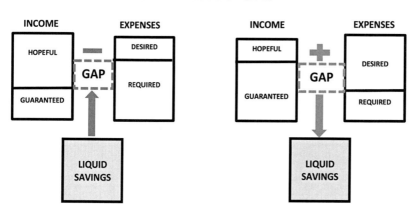

The final element to determine liquidity may be the most influential and important: your personal temperament. What amount of liquidity allows you to sleep at night? For most of us, emotion trumps logic. This paradigm cuts in both directions. Some people may hold greater-than-necessary reserves out of fear of the unknown and a lack of confidence in other liquidity options. Others may hold less than prudent levels of liquidity out of a false sense of security. In either case, the point is not to define your personal temperament as right or wrong, but rather to recognize what role our temperament plays and factor that into your decision on how much liquidity to maintain.

When planning your liquid reserve, it is prudent to establish a hierarchy of withdrawal sources. In other words, to which financial products will you allocate funds to serve as a portion of your liquid reserve and in which order will you access those sources? Several financial products can serve as sources for your liquidity needs: checking and savings accounts (don't forget to check out the online versions that often offer higher interest rates), money market accounts, brokerage accounts, certificates of deposit, annuities, and cash value life insurance. You may want to utilize different credit vehicles for some portion of your overall liquidity sources including credit cards and home equity lines of credit. Keep in mind, the power of compounding works in both directions. Don't compound your debt. When determining the order in which you access your different sources of liquidity, choose first the most liquid, least penalized (including the cost of interest on debt as a source of liquidity), lowest-yielding, least-taxed sources. You can create a hierarchy of withdrawals prior to ever needing to access the funds. By pre-planning, you bring more certainty to your retirement plans. You know you have sufficient liquidity and you know the order in which you will tap into that liquidity.

A portion of your overall liquid reserves may be allocated to what we term "crisis currency." Crisis currency can avert potential catastrophic events where either access to electronic payments (credit cards, debit cards, checks) or the value of the fiat currency is compromised. Crisis currency could include cash in your country's currency or that of other easily traded stable countries, precious metals like gold and silver (specifically in coins) and perhaps even cryptocurrency like Bitcoin or Ethereum. In a crisis scenario, how would you pay for essential expenses like food, fuel, or medical care? Keep cash and other crisis currency on hand in an amount that allows you to pass the "sleep at night" test. Keep your crisis currency in a location you will have easy access to, such as a home safe or home lockbox. Keeping your crisis currency in a safe deposit box at the bank is not a good idea because it may not be accessible during an emergency. Bankers typically discourage customers from keeping cash in safe deposit boxes because funds inside the box are not insured.

Got Money, Now What?

Arthur Godfrey, television pioneer and *Variety Show* host, once said, "*I am proud to pay taxes in the United States of America. The thing is, I could be just as proud for half the amount!*"

The next area of planning involves one of the two certainties in life—taxes. (The other is death.) We share Godfrey's sentiment in advising all our clients. Pay what is legally required, but always be looking to pay the least amount. In retirement, it truly is not what you make that counts but what you get to keep. As you will recall from chapter seven, you need to build your retirement planning team and a key member will be a tax strategist. Please note that a tax strategist may be a different person from your CPA, accountant, bookkeeper, or tax preparer. A simple analogy will reinforce this point. Is your tax professional a referee or a coach? A referee throws the flag and penalizes you while a coach teaches you how to win within the rules. The tax code has lots of rules as well as opportunities to minimize your tax bill in retirement. And while there is a myriad of tax issues that require advanced planning as you approach, enter, and pass through retirement, we are going to focus on the most common one, the one we believe is the most potentially impactful to you—your IRA.

Ticking Tax Time Bomb

When we reference the term IRA, we are including all pre-tax retirement plans including 401(k), 403(b), SEP, 457, Simple IRA, etc. We refer to these types of plans as ticking tax time bombs. The more you put into these plans and the longer they grow tax deferred, the greater the amount of taxes you or your beneficiaries will pay. And recent changes in the tax laws make passing your

IRA to your non-spouse beneficiaries less attractive. Uncle Sam has become your partner in your retirement account, giving you a tax deduction on your contributions in exchange for future taxation in an amount to be determined (tax rates can change) on your contributions *and* your gains. Sounds like Uncle Sam is buying low and selling high!

The good news is that you can minimize your tax bill while increasing certainty in retirement. One strategy to achieve these goals is known as a Roth conversion. The IRS tax code allows you to convert some or all your IRA funds to a Roth IRA. A traditional IRA is funded with pre-tax contributions, grows tax deferred, and is taxed as ordinary income when you withdraw the funds. A Roth IRA is funded with after-tax contributions, grows tax deferred, and can be withdrawn tax free. Your conversion can be done all at once or over several years. You can convert without penalty prior to reaching age fifty-nine-and-a-half. You must pay taxes on the amount converted for the tax year in which the conversion was completed.

UNCLE SAM'S PLAN IS NOT YOUR JAM

Would you rather pay taxes on the seed of your retirement savings (a smaller amount) at a known, and most likely lower, tax rate? Or would you rather pay taxes on the harvest of your retirement savings (a larger amount) at an unknown, but likely higher, tax rate? This demonstrates the potential power of Roth conversions. There are two phases of planning: having a conceptual understanding and crunching the numbers. For most clients, the option to complete a Roth conversion for at least a portion of their ticking tax time bomb is a no brainer. Clearly, the strategy is not right for everyone. However, the opportunity to pay the least amount of taxes combined with the certainty that your retirement savings will not be impacted by future tax rate increases for either you or your beneficiaries makes the strategy worthy of consideration.

So, how do you know whether a Roth conversion strategy is right for you? Here are some considerations:

1. Do you think taxes will go up, down, or remain the same? Understanding the current tax rates is imperative. At the writing of this book, we are at all-time historic low taxes, but they are scheduled to sunset in 2026. When they asked the infamous bank robber Willie Sutton why he robbed banks, his reply was classic: *"Because that's where the money is."* Taxing your IRA accounts is your government going where the money is. Most Americans believe that taxes are likely to go up based on the accelerating amount of our national debt. When you combine historic low tax rates, increases in government spending, and the already overwhelming and rapidly growing national debt, how could taxes not be raised significantly in the future?

2. Are your funds available for Roth conversion? Most IRA accounts are under your control and can be converted

upon your request. Other types of retirement accounts, particularly 401(k) and 403(b) plans, may not be readily available for conversion. If you have these types of accounts, check with your plan administrators to better understand your options. Note that many company-sponsored plans now allow you to convert traditional (pre-tax) accounts to Roth and to choose to contribute to either a traditional or Roth account within the plan. Your company matching contribution (if applicable) is normally added to your traditional account even if your contribution is made to the Roth account. Ask about the availability of in-service distributions or in-service transfers. In-service distributions allow you to withdraw funds from your company-sponsored 401(k) or 403(b) plan and transfer to your own IRA account. This allows you the ability to convert some or all the funds to a Roth IRA and be in control of choosing the underlying financial products.

3. Do you have access to funds outside of the IRA to pay the taxes on the Roth conversion? All funds converted will be potentially taxed as ordinary income in the tax year the conversion is completed. You must be able to cover this potential tax liability from funds that are outside your IRA accounts for this to be a smart option. It would not make financial sense to withdraw funds that will taxed (and perhaps penalized for pre-fifty-nine-and-a-half distribution) to pay taxes. With proper coordination with your tax strategist, you could allocate funds from your savings or increase the federal tax withholding on your paycheck to cover the taxes owed.

4. Do you know your tax bracket capacity for Roth conversions? You will need to work with your tax strategist

to determine your marginal tax rate and how much additional income you can add before moving into the next tax bracket, thereby increasing your marginal tax rate. This amount may vary year to year and should be forecasted by your tax strategist.

5. What are the best vehicles to use for the Roth conversion strategy? Although any IRA account can be converted to a Roth IRA, the underlying type of financial product can have an impact on the conversion and the amount of taxes paid. One of the primary watchouts involves converting assets that are volatile with respect to value over time. The amount of income included on your tax return for a Roth conversion is determined by the fair market value at the time of conversion. If the value decreases post conversion, you are still required to pay taxes on the higher amount converted. This could lead to paying taxes on losses, which most of us would agree is not a good plan. You may consider using a volatility buffer for the conversion period. We will discuss volatility buffer later in this chapter. Another technique that can further minimize the taxes paid on your Roth conversion is to convert "like kind" assets when they are lower. For example, if you owned 100 shares of Stock A, which you purchased at $100 per share or $10,000, and the current value of a share dropped to $50, you could convert your 100 shares with a fair market value of $5,000 (100 shares X $50 per share) and only pay taxes on the $5,000. When the share price goes back to $100 or higher, the entire gain is tax-free.

No Roth, No Worry

Recent changes to the IRA beneficiary rules eliminated the stretch IRA. A stretch IRA allowed a non-spouse beneficiary (think children or grandchildren) to stretch the payout from the IRA over their life expectancy. This minimized the amount of taxes paid and allowed the IRA to continue to grow over the lifetime of the beneficiary. Now non-spouse beneficiaries must withdraw the entire IRA balance over a maximum of ten years. Remember, Uncle Sam always gets paid first!

Many clients are choosing to use permanent cash value life insurance to overcome this ticking tax time bomb for their children and grandchildren. This can be especially true once required minimum distributions (RMD) kick in. RMD's were recently changed from age seventy-and-a-half to age seventy-two, delaying the mandatory starting date for withdrawals from IRA accounts by over a year. Many clients don't need or want to make withdrawals from their IRA accounts but must in order to comply or pay a significant penalty. You can utilize some or all your RMD (or withdraw prior to reaching the age of seventy-two in any amounts you choose) to purchase a tax-free death benefit guaranteed to remain in force for the rest of your life. This tax-free death benefit is paid directly to your designated beneficiaries, completely avoiding probate. Typically, clients can design plans that provide much higher amounts of death benefit compared to the current pre-tax value of their IRA accounts. Today's life insurance products are not your parents' boring, singularly focused insurance contracts. Today's life insurance can provide living benefits as well. Benefits can include access to cash value tax free, and advancing a portion of the death benefit each year for long-term care. In addition, the remaining balance of the IRA account is paid out to the beneficiaries and taxed appropriately.

What do the experts say about Roth conversions and life insurance? Ed Slott, one of America's leading IRA experts (and a veteran CPA of more than forty years) often compares homeownership with an IRA account. He notes that most retirees want to own their homes free and clear of a mortgage. IRA plans include a future tax burden that only grows over time. I don't know a single person who wants Uncle Sam as an equal partner in their retirement! Why not own your retirement plan free and clear of any future tax liability? You can pay off your IRA "mortgage" (the future tax liability owed to Uncle Sam) now by completing a Roth conversion. That same expert believes that the most powerful benefits in the tax code are provided for permanent life insurance. Leveraging those tax-free benefits passes more of your IRA to your kids tax free. In the end, both strategies will guarantee you and your beneficiaries pay the least amount of taxes and keep the most of your retirement savings.

Long-Term Care

They say death and taxes are the two certainties in life, but I believe we are close to having a third: long-term care. When it comes to long-term care, the numbers are overwhelming. First, the probability that you will require some type of long-term care services in your life is higher than every calamity other than death. Second, the financial (not to mention emotional) impact tends to be more devastating than an automobile accident or the loss of your home due to fire. But this higher probability of need and higher potential negative impact have not resulted in retirees purchasing traditional long-term care policies. Say what?

For a married couple turning sixty-five, there is a high probability at least one will need some type of long-term care in their life.

Christine Benz, in a 2021 report from Morningstar, states the following usage of long-term care statistics:

- 70%—people turning age sixty-five who will need some type of long-term-care services in their lifetimes.
- 48%—people turning age sixty-five who will need some type of paid long-term-care services in their lifetimes.
- 24%—people turning age sixty-five who will require paid long-term care for more than two years.
- 15%—people turning age sixty-five who will spend more than two years in a nursing home.
- 3.7 years—average duration of long-term-care need, women.
- 2.2 years—average duration of long-term-care need, men.
- 67.9%—people in long-stay nursing facilities who are women.

Not having a plan means you are on the default plan. You are planning to self-insure, rely on family, or turn to the government. For those clients who try to self-insure, most will exhaust their retirement savings and often impoverish their surviving spouse. Or worse yet, the caregiver ends up sicker or dies before the one receiving the care. Relying on your kids or other family members is the absolute last thing most retirees would want. The government options lack flexibility and do not necessarily provide the level of service and care we would want. They also require you to exhaust all your assets prior to receiving any assistance.

With all this data readily available and literally smacking Baby Boomers in the face, why don't most of us purchase a traditional long-term care policy? Because we hate thinking about needing long-term care. There are three major reasons why we don't buy a traditional long-term care policy:

UNCLE SAM'S PLAN IS NOT YOUR JAM

1. We don't want to pay a premium for something we may never use. Unlike auto or homeowner's insurance that may be required by law, we aren't forced to purchase coverage. Part of our belief is that we will never need long-term care; if we do, we will only need a little help from our spouse or family. They can handle it, right? What if you're wrong? Newsflash, the statistics confirm you are likely to be wrong. Most people won't consider long-term care until they or someone they know has had an experience taking care of a loved one. The reality of needing your kids to change your adult diapers is a powerful motivator.

2. We don't believe we can afford it. The price, especially if you start looking later in life, can be quite expensive and may be out of reach for many retirees. Couple this with the fact that traditional long-term care policies retain the right to increase premiums on policies and suddenly ongoing affordability becomes potentially questionable at best.

3. We can't qualify for the coverage. Many pre-retirees have medical conditions that would preclude them from receiving coverage. The irony is that these are the folks with the greatest probability of needing the protection offered by such coverage.

What's a concerned retiree to do? First, you need to have a plan even if that plan is self-insuring or relying on family. Discuss this plan up front with your spouse, partner, and family for agreement. Second, there are newer financial products that can provide benefits to help offset long-term care costs without purchasing a traditional long-term care policy. We are not dismissing traditional long-term care policies as a solution to this problem, but merely pointing out that it isn't an all-or-nothing choice. Most pre-retirees and retirees are looking for an alternative to traditional long-term care for one or all the reasons listed above.

Life Insurance: Death Benefit or Living Benefit or Both

Today, most permanent cash value life insurance policies offer a rider that allows you to advance the death benefit under certain conditions such as the need for long-term care services. The benefits of this type of plan for dealing with potential long-term care situations versus the traditional long-term care policy are many. First, it eliminates the first objection, paying for benefits you may never use. If you never need to use the policy for long-term care, the full amount of the death benefit is paid tax free to your beneficiaries. Second, the premiums can be more affordable and are guaranteed for life. Third, unlike a traditional long-term care policy where benefits are paid as reimbursement to licensed long-term care providers, these benefits are paid to you as cash that you can spend any way you desire, and you can pay anyone, including family members, to provide for your care.

The third obstacle to having a better long-term care plan remains the same for life insurance. You must be able to qualify medically. Don't let the perception of your health and your medical condition and how that might influence the insurance company keep you from investigating this possibility. Life insurance companies can differ tremendously on their underwriting requirements. What one company will refuse, another will insure. Today's insurers are more flexible in issuing coverage, and you may qualify. Make sure you are working with an independent expert who can shop the market to find the company that best matches your health profile. If you can't qualify or can't afford the premium, a similar long-term care benefit is now available on many annuity contracts that do not have strict medical requirements to qualify for potential long-term care benefits. This type of financial product can "multi-task" your retirement savings and help provide certainty for your retirement plans.

Sequence of Returns Trap

We know three things about the stock market: it goes up and down, it usually goes up over long periods of time, and stock investments often represent a significant portion of a retiree's retirement savings. As you progress along your financial life cycle, moving toward and through retirement, your tolerance and capacity for risk changes and the purpose of your money changes. As covered in chapter seven, the amount of risk you can accept generally goes down as the purpose for your money shifts from growth to preservation, income, and legacy. You will notice that as you shift your focus addressing your most important ROI (reliability of income) and create a positive certainty gap, it frees up the balance of your portfolio to achieve other goals and fulfill other purposes such as growth and legacy. Even though planning for guaranteed income leads to allocating a smaller portion of retirement savings to the stock market, most retirees will still have some amount at risk in stock market financial products and rely on the performance of these products to provide some portion of their desired expenses, and maybe even a portion of their required expenses. This may lead into the "sequence of returns" trap.

Losses Hurt More Than Gains Help

Sequence of returns is one of the most important concepts that retirees and pre-retirees should understand with respect to their retirement plan success. The order of investment returns can dramatically impact your retirement income. Financial professionals often speak about average returns, which can easily be misinterpreted as their forecast. The chart on page 156 provides an example of how averages can be deceiving. The sequence in which your investments experience gains, losses, and distributions can have major impact on the principal in your portfolio over time; this is consistent with the Monte Carlo Simulation.

The chart assumes that both retirees start with $100,000 and withdraw the same amount each year plus a cost-of-living increase. The sequence of return values is identical with one small change—the sequence is reversed from one portfolio to the other. Note the difference in the remaining balance between the two portfolios. The first portfolio results in the remaining balance being almost completely exhausted, while the second portfolio actually increases the balance. We refer to the first portfolio phenomenon as the "double-dip effect." The down-market distributions cannibalize your remaining balance at a much faster rate. The potential negative impact and implications of this double-dip effect can be devastating to your retirement plans. It may force you into uncomfortable decisions between maintaining the lifestyle you hoped for versus running out of money. Some Boomers may not have the choice to forego the down-market distribution because they need the funds to cover their required expenses or are forced to withdraw to fulfill their RMD (required minimum distributions). Even one year of market losses early in retirement may require significant adjustments to your plan. Conversely, the loss later in retirement will likely have much less of an impact. The implications from falling into the sequence-of-returns trap may force a downsize to your retirement lifestyle, risk impoverishing your spouse after your passing, or force one or both of you back into the workforce.

The conceptual solution to avoiding the sequence-of-returns trap is establishing a volatility buffer. A volatility buffer is achieved by allocating a portion of your retirement savings to financial products that are uncorrelated to market conditions. By design, the balances in these accounts do not go up and down with the market. The lack of volatility makes these accounts another source to withdraw from when the stock market is down and recovering. Once the stock market accounts have recovered, you can resume withdrawals from those type of accounts. Withdrawing from your volatility buffer accounts is perfect for the years the market goes down and the years the market is recovering. The biggest gains in a stock market account are often a result of the "bounce off the bottom." In other words, the flexibility provided by establishing a volatility buffer not only allows you to avoid the double-dip effect but also allows you to maximize your participation in the recovery from the market low point.

What type of financial products should you consider for establishing your volatility buffer? Consider any product that is not subject to fluctuating values and provides sufficient liquidity for the amount you may need or want to withdraw in a given year. Potential candidates would include savings accounts, money market accounts, fixed annuities, fixed indexed annuities, and cash value life insurance, each representing a different set of benefits and trade-offs.

Stealth Tax

We have all been subjected to a stealth tax, a tax so insidious and under the radar that few Americans even recognize it let alone fully comprehend the negative consequences on their financial

Portfolio 1: Experiences S&P 500 index returns from years 2000-2019

Portfolio 1		Assumption		$
Current Year	Historic S&P Year	S&P 20 Yr. Look-Back	IRA	IRA Dist.
Current Values		-	$100,000.00	-
2020	2000	-10.14%	$86,265.60	$4,000.00
2021	2001	-13.04%	$71,485.99	$4,060.00
2022	2002	-23.37%	$51,621.87	$4,120.90
2023	2003	26.38%	$59,953.60	$4,182.71
2024	2004	8.99%	$60,716.31	$4,245.45
2025	2005	3.00%	$58,099.39	$4,309.14
2026	2006	13.62%	$61,043.05	$4,373.77
2027	2007	3.53%	$58,601.78	$4,439.38
2028	2008	-38.49%	$33,274.33	$4,505.97
2029	2009	23.45%	$35,431.10	$4,573.56
2030	2010	12.78%	$34,723.76	$4,642.16
2031	2011	0.00%	$30,011.97	$4,711.80
2032	2012	13.41%	$28,612.77	$4,782.47
2033	2013	29.60%	$30,791.10	$4,854.21
2034	2014	11.39%	$28,809.99	$4,927.02
2035	2015	-0.73%	$23,635.26	$5,000.93
2036	2016	9.54%	$20,329.87	$5,075.94
2037	2017	19.42%	$18,125.32	$5,152.08
2038	2018	-6.24%	$12,091.25	$5,229.36
2039	2019	28.88%	$8,742.51	$5,307.80
		5.60%	$8,742.51	$92,494.67

Portfolio 2: Experiences S&P 500 index returns from years 2019-2000 (reversed)

Portfolio 2		Assumption		$
Current Year	Historic S&P Year	S&P 20 Yr. Look-Back	IRA	IRA Dis
Current Values		-	$100,000.00	-
2020	2019	28.88%	$123,724.80	$4,000.0
2021	2018	-6.24%	$112,197.72	$4,060.0
2022	2017	19.42%	$129,065.33	$4,120.9
2023	2016	9.54%	$136,796.42	$4,182.7
2024	2015	-0.73%	$131,583.35	$4,245.4
2025	2014	11.39%	$141,770.74	$4,309.1
2026	2013	29.60%	$178,066.47	$4,373.7
2027	2012	13.41%	$196,910.49	$4,439.3
2028	2011	0.00%	$192,404.52	$4,505.9
2029	2010	12.78%	$211,835.75	$4,573.9
2030	2009	23.45%	$255,780.49	$4,642.
2031	2008	-38.49%	$154,432.35	$4,711.8
2032	2007	3.53%	$154,932.52	$4,782.4
2033	2006	13.62%	$170,518.98	$4,854.
2034	2005	3.00%	$170,559.71	$4,927.4
2035	2004	8.99%	$180,442.52	$5,000.
2036	2003	26.38%	$221,628.28	$5,075.
2037	2002	-23.37%	$165,885.71	$5,152.4
2038	2001	-13.04%	$139,706.76	$5,229.
2039	2000	-10.14%	$120,770.90	$5,307.
		5.60%	$120,770.90	$92,494

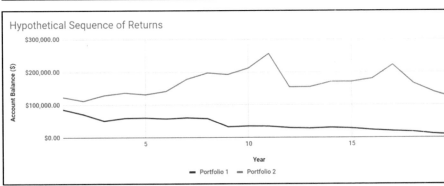

Hypothetical Sequence of Returns

umptions in the examples:

100,000 initial investment

4,000 annual withdrawals (increasing 1.5% each year for inflation)

ctual S&P 500 index returns for years 2000-2019

le both examples have the same average return (5.6%) and the same
idrawals ($92,494.67), the ending account balance for Portfolio 2 is more
1 ten times larger than Portfolio 1. Portfolio 1 will have a more difficult
: providing retirement income due to its sequence of returns.

ucing the impact of down markets

·ffective way to reduce the negative impact in Portfolio 1 is to have sources
come that are not vulnerable to the unpredictability of the markets. There
options available that can provide guaranteed principal protection. There
also options that can provide a guaranteed stream of income. Please consult
your financial professional for additional advice on these options.

erstanding the dangers of using past averages to predict future growth is
·ly important. This should be a discussion item as it will help protect you
i relying on overly bullish market performance recommendations. If you
:ve your investments could experience a series of down market years, be
to make this topic a priority when speaking with your financial
essionals.

ember, we have enjoyed a historically long bull market. While COVID-19 had
matic negative impact on the stock markets, the markets did recover very
<ly. The "V" shape we have witnessed may be giving us a false sense of
rity. This coronavirus disrupted so much of the world's economy; is it
ible it's all behind us?

Retirement
Architecture

well-being. I am, of course, referring to inflation. Inflation is not due to evil corporations raising their prices but rather the devaluing of our currency by government-aligned entities. The Federal Reserve is neither federal nor a reserve. It is a private central bank empowered by our government to print a fiat currency (backed only by the promise to pay, from the federal government, rather than a true source of value like gold or silver) and to set the intrabank lending rates that ultimately impact our consumer rates. To learn more about the history of the Federal Reserve, read *The Creature from Jekyll Island* by G. Edward Griffin. The ability of our government to hide the truth from the American citizen and taxpayer it is supposed to represent, continues to amaze. So, what's the big deal about inflation?

There is a perfect storm organizing around inflation and its impact on your retirement plans. We are living longer and spending more years in retirement than any generation before us. This enhances—in a negative direction—the compounding effects of rising prices for goods and services. The national debt is expanding at a rate that places the solvency of our country at risk. This overwhelming level of debt contributes to inflation as the Fed tries to ease our economy out of recession by increasing the money supply. The fact that many retirees are on fixed incomes can be like an unforeseen financial tsunami. Unlike the days when we worked in our careers and could receive pay raises and promotions, we must figure out how to deal with stagnant fixed incomes and rising expenses. And what about the potential impact of long-term care? It's not a pretty picture, is it?

Do nothing and you will be a victim of inflation. It can turn your positive certainty gap into a negative certainty gap. It can cause you to downsize your retirement dreams. It can force you into difficult decisions regarding where you want to live and the medical care you can afford. It may even send you back to the workforce. Working in retirement because you love what you do is not the same as working because you must. What can you do to prevent the perfect storm from destroying your retirement blueprint? Let's review our options.

You can plan your guaranteed sources of income to include cost-of-living or other increasing income benefits. Social Security includes a cost-of-living increase each year (sometimes it inexplicably is zero). If you have a pension, often your payout options offer a cost-of-living benefit. If you are creating your own pension by using an annuity product, many of the options for lifetime guaranteed income can include increasing income benefits. You can create an Income Ladder by purchasing future income financial products that provide additional layers of income at some future point in time. You can manage your volatility buffer to allow withdrawals to supplement your other sources of income. You could plan to withdraw from your liquid reserve to supplement your retirement paycheck. You could utilize stock market accounts to serve as your supplemental income during your later years of retirement. You can allocate a portion of your retirement savings to products that offer the opportunity for growth like stocks, real estate, precious metals or cryptocurrency. Make a better plan for yourself today.

Love It or List It

One of my favorite real estate shows is the popular HGTV series, *Love It or List It*. The show features a different couple each episode. One of them wants to move out of their current problematic house into a new home; the other wants to remodel their current house, transforming it into their new forever home. When you retire, you may face a similar "love it or list it" moment. Think of your own home, where you raised your children through all those holidays and memorable events. Close your eyes and you can still see the pencil marks on the door frame capturing height and age over the years for your own children. But over time, "home sweet home" can morph into a "dungeon of distress." And instead of being the king or queen of your castle, you are now the servant indentured to the homestead you once loved. What happened?

We got older and so did our homes. Our desire and ability to continue to maintain the old home has decreased at the same time our house needs more loving care—a new roof, air conditioning, water heater, flooring, updated appliances, and on and on. The house that was just right for you, your spouse, and kids has now become more than you need, not to mention more than you want to clean. And those stairs! You know it's time to make a change when you strategically plan each trip up or down the stairs to minimize the stress on your knees. Why are we so reluctant to leave? To move onto something new and better suited for our current physical and financial life cycle? It's probably because we are creatures of habit and gravitate to that which is known and comfortable. Change is one of the most difficult things to do, and even more so when it involves a new address with new surroundings, new neighbors, and new routines. Don't let the devil you know keep you from pursuing your best retirement path, even if it means moving from your current home. Besides, your kids probably don't want to keep your house after you are gone.

The Upside of Downsizing

My mother-in-law downsized from a hundred-year-old, two-story house to a new one-level, low-maintenance home that more than met her needs. She was an incredible mid-western scratch cook, so she needed a big kitchen. She needed plenty of closet space for her treasures and extra bedrooms for frequent guests. She was able to live comfortably on her own until passing at the age of ninety-one. She gave up some space along with the stairs, high utility bills, lots of repairs and maintenance. But she didn't miss the worry of something else needing to be replaced. Her new home gave her more certainty, less maintenance, lower utility bills, and therefore more peace of mind. How do you know if it's time to move? What is your living plan for the no-go years? What are you waiting for?

Rent versus Own

Many retirees are choosing to "list it" and rent rather than own. They like transferring the risk of home ownership to companies that manage the risk and accept the responsibility for maintenance and repairs and replacing appliances when necessary. One call to place a work order and it's done within a day or two. Rental communities often have plenty of extra amenities like pools, spas, gyms, pet parks, and clubhouses with activities such as bridge, dominos, and other games. Some have conference rooms with office support. Choosing this option allows you to sell your old home and use the funds to create more guaranteed sources of income, creating a bigger retirement paycheck.

If you choose to move, downsizing and estate sale experts can be a tremendous help. We recently downsized and it was the most wonderful experience. My only job was to go through our belongings and pack what we wanted to keep. We did not have to touch any other items. We were instructed to leave *anything* we didn't want to take with us, including half-used bottles of shampoo and spices. The estate sale company arrived after we moved our belongings and set up our home for display. The sale took a few days; on the last day, they donated anything remaining to charitable organizations. I felt this was a win/win/win for all involved. Here is what I learned: The stuff we think has value really doesn't matter. It is all about the experiences we associate with things, and those experiences live in our heart.

When I moved to Florida from Pennsylvania, I brought with me a few sets of china and hand-painted Italian dinnerware, with place settings for eight and sixteen. What was I thinking? I had moved to Florida. If sixteen people were coming for dinner, we would be eating in the lanai on paper plates (of course they would be high-quality paper plates, but disposable nevertheless). I don't think I used our formal dining room more than three times in eighteen years. It has been a few years since we downsized, and I can't think of a single thing I wish I had hung onto.

Reverse Mortgages

A reverse mortgage may be an option if you choose to "love it." A reverse mortgage is like a "forward" mortgage or a loan on your property. With a traditional mortgage, you pay principal and interest every month, thereby reducing the amount of outstanding debt on your home. With a reverse mortgage, you never make mortgage payments. Instead, the amount of interest on the loan is added to your loan balance each month until you sell the home. At that time, the original mortgage plus the accrued interest is paid. A reverse mortgage has safeguards built in that ensure you (or your heirs) are never upside down on the property. In other words, you will never owe more than the property is worth. This product can be a great tool for the retiree who plans on staying in their home, has significant equity, and needs to increase cash flow. It isn't right for everyone, but it may allow you to stay in your home if that is what you desire.

Continuing Care Communities

AARP highlights continuing care retirement communities, also known as CCRC's or life plan communities. It provides a solid list of key questions to ask if you are considering this option. CCRC's are a long-term care option for older people who want to stay in the same property and with the same management through different phases of the aging process. Your loved one needs to be involved in the selection process.

LeadingAge, a nationwide organization of nonprofit and government aging-services providers, recommends that prospective residents ask these ten key questions when considering a continuing care retirement community:

1. Are you for-profit or not-for-profit, and what's the financial strength of the retirement community?
2. What's included in the monthly fee?
3. How do you help residents maintain freedom and independence?
4. What kind of emergency response systems do you have?
5. How do you measure residents' satisfaction? Can I see your last two surveys?
6. How can residents offer input and feedback?

7. What is the difference between independent and assisted living; when would someone move to assisted living?
8. Can someone remain in independent living when their needs change, and how is aging in place supported?
9. What are the five most popular programs in your community, and who decides what programs and events are scheduled?
10. Can we review your residency agreement?

The nation's nearly 2,000 CCRC's offer different types of housing and care levels based on a senior's changing needs. A resident can start out living independently in an apartment and later transition to assisted living to get more help with daily activities or to skilled nursing to receive more medical care while remaining in the same community.

The chief benefit of CCRC's is that they provide a wide range of care, services, and activities in one place, offering residents a sense of stability and familiarity as their abilities or health conditions change. But that comes at a cost.

Nearly two-thirds of the communities charge an entry fee, according to a study from commercial real estate services firm CBRE Group Inc.. The average initial payment is $329,000, but it can top $1 million at some communities. Once residents move in, they pay monthly maintenance or service fees that typically run $2,000 to $4,000. Other continuing care communities operate on a rental model with no up-front fee. Rent for an independent living unit is often $3,000 to $6,000 a month.

Moving in With Children

Moving in with your children may be a win/win option to consider. The win for them is having you around to support their growing family. Instilling family values is priceless. They may have the ability to construct in-law quarters, and there are even companies that specialize in "Prefab Granny Pods" that can be delivered and installed in your children's back yard. They are about the size of a hotel room. They are also called ADUs, or accessory dwelling units, and are designed with safety and accessibility top of mind (for example, slip-resistant floors, wide doorways, and rounded countertops). Some versions offer high-tech medical extras. Another reason to consider alternative long-term care solutions; some will allow the benefit to pay for this option.

Decluttering

Marie Kondo is a tidying expert, bestselling author, and star of Netflix's hit show, *Tidying Up with Marie Kondo*, and yes, I got hooked on her show. I *loved* her famous question: "When you pick up an item, does it bring you joy?" It is really that simple. All the clothes I kept because one day, eventually, I would lose the weight and they would fit again? They only brought me feelings of failure. A funny thing happened when I released them to the estate sale. I finally released those extra pounds I had been carrying around for years. And no, I didn't ever wish I had kept any of those clothes! Whether you have watched Marie Kondo or not, there are plenty of decluttering experts around. You can hire one to help you sort your treasures.

Begin passing on your family heirlooms while you are alive. Who says you must wait until you pass? I don't know if you are like me, but

I find that as I age, I rarely wear jewelry and tend to use the same few purses and totes. Isn't there a loved one in your family who would adore a vintage "whatever" now? How cool to be around to experience their joy. If they don't have the same appreciation for the item, donate it to someone who will find value. Isn't that a more positive energy than your loved ones rummaging through your stuff after you pass?

> *Not having a plan is a plan...the government default plan!*
> *Do you really want Uncle Sam as an equal partner in your retirement?*
>
> *~Judi Snyder*

Choosersizes – Give Less to the IRS

🐚 Determine liquidity needs and hierarchy of withdrawals using the sequence of returns.

🐚 Evaluate your Roth options and decide whether this option is appropriate for a portion of your IRA money.

🐚 Define and begin to set up a long-term care plan and weigh your housing options in preparation for the no-go years.

*Download the companion workbook
www.BecomingRetiredishWorkbook.com

SUMMARY

Fabtastic! You made this journey with me until the end (unless you are like my husband Jeff, who reads the end of every book first). Did you know that only five percent of people who read books make it past the first chapter? Although this book may not be a steamy, sexy novel, it does hold the promise for lasting joy and fulfillment in your retiredish years.

Section one was all about your purpose and focused on your inner self, the part of you that may have been neglected your entire life. This can be illuminating. The importance of learning your driving values or your inner spirituality, your "big why," provides you with direction and helps you make decisions that serve you. Understanding how limiting beliefs prevent you from moving forward on your why is imperative and necessary if you want to get unstuck when life happens. What good is knowing your big why if you live in a state of paralysis or stuckness? Once you're able to eliminate the negative energy of limiting beliefs that hold you back, you are free to choose a life you love—maybe for the first time. You begin to recognize your gifts and appreciate and learn from your blunders.

Section two addressed wellness, but not necessarily in the style of a health guru. Instead, we focused on the challenges of the retiredish population. It is important to become aware of how you can optimize your experiences despite any physical limitations you are likely to experience as you age. There are a million books about diet and exercise by some phenomenal experts, if you want to go deeper into optimizing your physical health. We focused heavily on forgiveness and grief because in retirement, those are the two most deadly predators to your happiness. Regret is a killer of joy; if we don't get a handle on it, we are doomed to live a joyless life. I don't want that journey for anyone. Rounding out section two we learned what most people consider the key to peace of mind—knowing their loved ones would be taken care of and happy. The B.Y.E. List is love in action. Having all your important documents accessible and detailed provides your loved ones with peace at a time when their grief is the most intense and they are the least able to make good decisions.

Section three addresses your money. Although money isn't the most important thing about retirement, it does provide you more choices and hey, this entire book is about choices. I wanted to include the areas I was unaware of about money even though I was considered a "finance diva" in my corporate days. Knowing how to make money does not guarantee you will know what to do with it once you have it. Understanding your most important ROI, your certainty gap, and the predators to your retirement paycheck and playcheck, help you put plans in place so you can enjoy "sleep equity."

On a final note, I have a confession. I almost didn't publish my book because I got "stuck" in 2020 navigating the year of Covid-19, lockdowns, and contentious politics. I'm a flaming extrovert and the isolation and lack of connection just about killed me. I felt like an imposter; how could I position myself as an expert when I was stuck? When my husband encouraged me to go through my book as a reader, not a writer, and repeat my Choosersizes, a funny thing happened. Not *ha-ha* funny, but ironic funny. I learned some new things about myself, things that might not have surfaced had it not been for 2020. I was able to embrace the "yuk" of 2020, pick myself up, and course correct my attitude more easily than I had in the past during difficult times. I was able to appreciate the awakening and clarity 2020 gifted me and adjust my life accordingly. Once you have a framework, it speeds the process of finding joy again. I can guarantee that challenges will continue to come up in all areas of life. By taking the time now to develop your personal framework for dealing with challenges, you will equip yourself with the mindset and tools to correct your course in the heat of the moment.

My experience reminded me of two of my favorite analogies. The first is a quote from the late Jim Rohn who said, *"Listen carefully but don't look too closely. I'm working on this stuff too!"* I have learned it is easy to teach and share good ideas for others in their *Becoming Retiredish* journey, but not always easy to do yourself. For this reason, I recommend a "thought partner" or accountability partner to support you when course correction is needed. The second is an analogy we have used countess times to describe the retirement planning experience from pre-retirement all the way through to your eventual passing. We compare this journey to a flight from New York to Los Angeles and highlight the fact that for most of the flight, the plane is off course. But because the plane makes frequent adjustments, it ends up at the intended destination. If the plane were off course by only a few degrees, it would land in Mexico City. Now, I'm not saying that Mexico City is a bad place to end up, it just wasn't the intended destination. Furthering the analogy, the plane often experiences unexpected turbulence and must adjust, flying thru, over, below, or around the problem weather. The comparisons to your retirement planning journey are strikingly similar. Whether it is purpose, wellness, or money, this is not a one-and-done process. And just like boarding a plane and going through the safety requirements, you must put your oxygen mask on first before helping others. Any good plan requires an annual or at least regular review to confirm your needs are being properly met.

We covered a lot of material in this book and the Choosersizes require an investment of time, honest answers, and contemplation. Your investment of time and emotional capital will yield significant dividends by providing both the framework and emotional resilience to navigate your trip successfully and happily, from the go-go years to the slow-go years to the no-go years. I wish you a joyful and abundant Retiredish journey.

To connect with me, visit my website www.BecomingRetiredish.com

ABOUT THE AUTHOR

**Judi Snyder CeFT®, CPRC, Author, Speaker,
Financial Transition and Retirement Coach**

Twenty-seven years as a medical sales executive led Judi to realize that corporate life was unfulfilling. In 2004 she transitioned from employee to entrepreneur into financial services. Because of her own transition, she understands the unique challenges that come along with creating a new identity and purpose. Judi became a CeFT® (Certified Financial Transitionist®) to further expand her toolbox of solutions for those going through financial transition and help her address the financial aspects of transition. She helps clients navigate through the non-financial aspects of retirement— finding purpose, exploring spirituality, and health and wellness— which are as important as financial planning yet rarely addressed. Becoming a CPRC (Certified Professional Retirement Coach) further expanded her tool chest with solutions to holistically guide those in or approaching retirement. Happiness and fulfillment are about more than the money.

JUDI SNYDER
CeFT®, CPRC

FINALLY... IT'S YOUR TIME TO CHOOSE A LIFE YOU LOVE

BECOMING RETIRED*ish*

A GUIDE FOR THE NEARLY OR NEWLY RETIRED

JUDI SNYDER CeFT®, CPRC

...nternationally recognized retirement transition coach, Judi Snyder helps ...ple nearing or in retirement, find ...ose, wellness, and financial certainty in ...retired-ish years.

...understands the unique challenges ... come along with creating a new ...ity and purpose, completing her own ...ition from corporate employee to an ...preneur in financial services in 2004.

...became a Certified Financial ...sitionist® (CeFT®) and a Certified ...essional Retirement Coach (CPRC), ...nding her tool chest to help clients ...ate through both the financial and ...inancial aspects of retirement, such as ...ng purpose, exploring spirituality, ...h and wellness.

...ngaging and down to earth speaker, ...leaves her audiences empowered to ...control and create joy in their retired-...ars.

BECOMING RETIRED*ish*

A GUIDE FOR THE NEARLY OR NEWLY RETIRED

- It's about more than money, but getting money right gives you more choices.

- How discovering purpose can finally give you the joy you deserve.

- The number one thing that is affecting your health, and it isn't diet and exercise!

- How to make decisions that may be difficult for those you love, ahead of time, so your loved ones won't be burdened with them during their grief.

- Your most important ROI is not what you think! Understanding the top predators to your financial freedom.

PROFESSIONAL DESIGNATIONS   Financial Transitionist® Institute

Judi@HomeStretchFinancial.com   www.HomeStretchFinancial.com

173

FOR YOU!

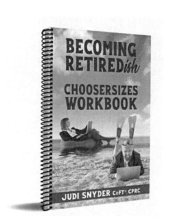

Want more?

Download your complimentary companion workbook jam-packed with "Choosersizes" (exercises for retiredish people who want to choose a life they love) to guide you on your journey of becoming retiredish.

The *Retiredish Workbook* is custom-designed for the readers of *Becoming Retiredish,* created to maximize your own personal success. Use this guide to support your journey of transitioning from *shoulding* to *choosing* a life of purpose, wellness, and financial certainty in your retiredish years.

VISIT HERE TO DOWNLOAD YOUR COPY
www.RetiredishWorkbook.com

Visit our website www.HomeStretchFinancial.com for additional up-to-the-minute online education videos and eBooks all designed to give you the power of choice at your fingertips.

For a limited time, you will be able to book a 30-minute *Becoming Retiredish* strategy session to discuss your personal circumstances and determine your individual support opportunities.

We are experts at creating certainty in your retiredish years!

Visit www.BecomingRetiredish.com to book your obligation-free session.

ACKNOWLEDGMENTS

I must first acknowledge Jeff Snyder, my husband and business partner, who demystified numbers and spreadsheets and transformed my personal finance expertise. Jeff was instrumental in the financial section of *Becoming Retiredish*. His superpower is making complex concepts easy to comprehend and, most of all, actionable. I would also like to acknowledge my mother-in-law, Doris Snyder, who raised a man of integrity, compassion, humor, and Euchre superiority that is unmatched. She had been a second Mom and had offered love and support to me from the moment I met her.

I also want to acknowledge my friends, clients, and colleagues who have uniquely contributed to my personal and professional growth that led to the information and insights I share in this book. I'll start with my childhood bestie and cousin, Marianne J. We were inseparable as children, and I learned about the meaning and value of true friendship at an early age.

My "Regina Hall Rebels" college friends were definitely "Catholic girls who started much too late." (Thanks, Billy Joel, for that one.) But we caught up, and we still get together every year to celebrate our friendship.

My BFF, Andee S., is definitely one of "those" friends. She would not bail me out of jail because she would be in jail with me. With Andee's unconditional love and support, I've been able to navigate life's challenges and celebrate life's gifts for forty-five years.

My Tampa Bay "Lolitas" have been together almost since the week I moved to Florida in 1998 and truly define all that sisterhood represents. I am grateful every day for these five beautiful and accomplished women who have helped each other navigate the corporate world and have seen each other through middle age and beyond.

I'm grateful to my bestie and sales and marketing doppelganger, Barrie P., for highlighting the path to writing this book and for being a superb accountability partner. Finally, I want to acknowledge Marianne I. We met my first day of college and with her I've learned several lifetimes worth of insight about myself, my values, and my relationships.

NOTES